# GOVERNMENT IS THE PROBLEM

**How to change the conditions on the political battlefield and win back America**

COLONEL PATRICK MURRAY

*AuthorHouse™*
*1663 Liberty Drive*
*Bloomington, IN 47403*
*www.authorhouse.com*
*Phone: 1 (800) 839-8640*



*Published by AuthorHouse 05/14/2015*

*ISBN: 978-1-4969-6978-1 (sc)*
*ISBN: 978-1-4969-6977-4 (e)*

*Print information available on the last page.*



*This book is printed on acid-free paper.*

# DEDICATION

To single mothers, including mine, who look into the eyes of their child and find a way. Flora Mae, I'm honored to be your son.

# CONTENTS

# FOREWORD

"I fight authority, authority always wins."
–John Cougar Mellencamp

I believe that God looks out for us with a deity-sized sense of humor. I'd worked countless jobs growing up; slinging newspapers off of my Schwinn, pouring concrete, flipping burgers, mowing lawns, selling clothes, insulating houses, and the list goes on. What I was really good at though, was getting into and out of trouble. I didn't have a clue about what I was going to do when I "grew up," but I knew that I was allergic to anything resembling authority, authority figures, rules, regulations, laws, orders, homework, or whatever; get thee behind me. God bless my mom, a single mother who loved and stuck by her unruly kid. She always told me there was something out there for me, something I'd feel led to do. I can honestly say that the last thing on my mind was anything involving uniforms and saluting. But one morning there I was, jarred awake at 3:00 a.m. by a trashcan-lid-banging drill sergeant in Fort Knox, Kentucky. Oh yeah, I'd joined the U.S. Army. Deity-sized sense of humor indeed, but the Big Guy upstairs absolutely had my back. The army changed my life, gave me a firm sense of purpose and the knowledge that I was part of something significant, something bigger than myself. Perhaps most important, serving all over the world afforded me a powerful sense of perspective and the realization of how good I had it simply by virtue of having been born in the greatest country in history. I took an oath to support and defend the Constitution of the United States against all enemies, foreign and domestic, and I was honored to do that for twenty-five years. Army life is behind me now, but there is no statute of limitations on that oath. We owe it to future generations to forever support and defend this unique experiment of limited government and individual liberty that is America—even when our own government becomes the problem. A quote often attributed to Thomas Jefferson reads, "A government big enough to give you everything you want is a government big enough to take everything you have." I guess I still have issues with authority, especially when that authority oversteps its bounds and turns into a bully. We know that the best way to deal with a bully is a punch in the nose. And that's exactly what an Article V-based Convention of States will deliver to an oppressive government and to career politicians who are destroying the American Dream.

Love your country, not your government.

# INTRODUCTION

"All tyranny needs to gain a foothold is for people of good conscience to remain silent."
–Edmund Burke

This book began as an after action review following the 2012 elections. Like millions of other conservatives, I was concerned for our nation's future in the wake of Obama's reelection. My intent was to vent my frustrations with the Republican Party and to find a way forward that would return America to its constitutional roots of limited government, individual liberty, and a free market economy. I also had some personal skin in the game that went beyond my patriotism. In 2009, after twenty-five years serving in the United States Army, I decided to leave the armed forces and run for the US Congress. My family, friends, and fellow soldiers wondered why an otherwise sane individual would make such a career choice. Here's why.

In 2008 I was a Colonel serving in the U.S. Mission to the United Nations as the Department of Defense representative for Arms Control, and Security Council issues at the UN. When Obama won the election that year, I was tasked by the Office of the Secretary of Defense to facilitate their transition on U.S. defense-related issues at the UN. For years preceding that, the Bush Administration, and my old boss Ambassador John Bolton, had held the line at the UN in defense of U.S. national security interests. For example, in the arms control arena it was our policy to stress the importance of nuclear nonproliferation, particularly with regard to bad actors like Iran and Islamist extremist groups like al-Qaeda who would like nothing better than to get their hands on a nuclear weapon and detonate it in Tel Aviv, New York, or Washington, DC, killing millions. To us and to our close allies like Israel this nightmare scenario posed a major threat to international security and stability. No brainer, right? Well not so much, actually. The balance of the UN universe wanted a very different conversation, one that focused disarmament, particularly with regard to the United States and our nuclear arsenal. For them, our existing capability was as every bit the threat to global stability than the potential for Iran or al-Qaeda to acquire nukes. Such is the mentality at the United Nations where the United States is appreciated for its money, but little else. By the way, American tax dollars comprise the single biggest funding source for the UN.

However, in the wake of the 2008 presidential election, a new sheriff was riding into town. The fledgling Obama regime was eager to prove that there was nothing particularly exceptional about America, that we were just another country, in fact there was substantial head nodding that American strength was a problem, a source of instability in the world. So the plethora of multilateral initiatives such as the International Criminal Court, Kyoto Protocols, Law of the Sea, Weaponization of outer space, and the Arms Trade Treaty (a backdoor way to limit the Second Amendment), all arguably designed to constrain American power and wealth by chipping away at our sovereignty were now in play. Moreover, the Obama team was quick to align itself with the nuclear disarmament crowd, something that concerned me deeply.

For the first time in my military career, I found myself strongly opposed to the actions of my own government. I also disagreed with what they were doing on the domestic front: the trillion-dollar "shovel-ready" job stimulus program, Obamacare, tax hikes, demonizing the private sector, and empowering a government already big and powerful enough to wipe your nose and brush your teeth. Apparently this was all part of Obama's stated goal to "fundamentally transform America." In my view, the only reason to fundamentally transform anything is because you believe it to be tragically flawed. Really, Barack? America tragically flawed? It became clear to me that I could no longer in good conscience salute and carry out the orders and initiatives of an administration that seemed determined to repudiate America's exceptional nature, and pursue policies opposed to our national interests. So I reluctantly dropped my retirement paperwork and said good-bye to the army.

Military service is as challenging as it is rewarding. Wearing the uniform is a constant reminder that you are a part of something important, something bigger than yourself. It starts with taking that oath to "support and defend the Constitution against all enemies, foreign and domestic." For me that oath of office didn't expire when I took off the cloth of my country, so stepping into the political arena was just another way to fulfill that oath. More important, it was an avenue of approach to confronting and influencing policy from the inside that I saw as part of the problem. Or so I thought.

I ran twice: in 2010 and 2012. Both times we won the primaries but lost the in general elections. It was disappointing to lose, but I ran in a very tough district for someone of my political flavor; there hasn't been a Republican representing the Eighth District of Virginia since Christ was a corporal. Still, I believed voters deserved a choice, so I ran, and was honored to twice be the party nominee. I harbor no regrets and will forever be proud of the high integrity with which we ran our campaigns and the honest message we delivered, even when it was not at all what most voters of my district wanted to hear. I had zero political experience, which many viewed as a plus, although the party establishment types seemed threatened by an "outsider." However I came fully equipped with the values of duty, honor, and country that all soldiers live, breathe, and operate by. I was honored to serve alongside some amazing volunteers and salt-of-the-earth patriots. And in the end, everything happens for a reason; one door closes while another one opens. Thus this book.

That experience of being steeped inside of American politics at the national level was an eye-opener. I learned a great deal about what goes on in Congress and in Washington. Things like who really wins and who really loses. It was a "look behind the curtain" into the reality of politicians, parties, and government. As a veteran and as an American, I was disturbed by what I saw. The sense of selfless service, leadership, integrity, and honor that is commonplace in the military was largely AWOL in Congress.

Whatever your politics, it is easy to cast the entire blame for America's shortfalls on the other side. In fact that's about all Republicans and Democrats do, every minute of every day. It is how they raise money, how they become known, how they get on TV, how they get reelected. It had also been my default approach for some time—Democrats wore the black hats and Republicans wore the white hats. But it just isn't that simple.

The Constitution constrained government and concurrently maximized individual liberty. Thomas Jefferson defined liberty as "unobstructed action according to our will within limits drawn around us by the equal rights of others. I do not add 'within the limits of the law' because law is often but the tyrant's will, and will always so when it violates the rights of the individual."[1] That last clause that Jefferson felt compelled to include looks very prescient right about now. That's because the respective roles of government and individuals have flipped. Government power, and its ability to act against Main Street America, is virtually unlimited. Rule of law

1 http://www.brainyquote.com/quotes/quotes/t/thomasjeff136362.html?src=t_liberty.

is becoming the government's will; it has the power, capability, and authority to willfully, in Jefferson's words, "violate the rights of the individual." It is a massive parasite that is draining Main Street America in order to sustain and expand. We, the people are the hosts, and we exist under a deluge of ever-expanding laws, rules, and regulations. Career politicians pass laws that coerce dependency upon the government in a zero-sum game that saps our initiative and innate desire for self-betterment. We are kept in check by weaponized government agencies and departments, a.k.a. "Power Ministries" (see chapter 3) that monitor our movements, listen to our phone calls, and read and record every e-mail, text, or tweet we send out. It is as if we are all living inside the lyrics of that creepy Police song: "Every breath you take, every move you make… every word you say… I'll be watching you." We all know what a gigabyte is. Try terabytes and petabytes; that's the storage currency our government operates in. "Metadata" is Orwell on steroids.

It's tempting for conservatives to dump all of the blame for big government, high taxes, federal debt, etc., on Democrats. After all, liberals openly advocate for a nanny state, higher taxes, government-dictated social justice, Kumbayah. I wholeheartedly agree with that observation; in fact chapter 3 of this book will explain how progressivism has poisoned American political culture. But what I know now is that it isn't that simple; America's problems do not begin and end with liberals (who, I would note, fall all over themselves blaming Republicans for everything wrong). The reality in America today is that we endure a class of career politicians *of both parties* who aren't in Congress to support and defend the Constitution; they are there to support and defend their incumbencies and to grow government. They've broken the code that their political longevity, influence, and personal wealth are inexorably intertwined with a powerful, expansive federal government. Therefore, in my view, the real chasm in America, and the real battle *for* America, isn't Left vs. Right; it is Washington vs. Main Street.

Politicians, Democrat and Republican alike, will say and do whatever it takes to stay in office, and they have rigged the system such that their reelection is almost always predetermined. And they understand all too well that bigger, more powerful federal government is an extension of their own personal power and job security. The longer they spend in Washington the more powerful and wealthy they become. What's worse, lawmakers are made of Kevlar when it comes to avoiding responsibility for their actions. Break laws, bounce checks, "forget" to pay your taxes, use secret government briefings for insider trading, pick winners and losers in the private sector and get payoffs through corrupt, crony capitalism, whatever. And when they do decide to leave office, they take their taxpayer-funded government pensions and Cadillac health-care plans with them, and walk across the street into lucrative lobbying jobs in the plush office suites that populate Capitol Hill. Even there, *especially* there, the expansion of government translates into huge payoffs and job security. They aren't called "beltway bandits" for nothing. Chapter 2 addresses career politicians, how they are harming America and, sadly, how, in my opinion, that Republican complicity is in many ways more detrimental than that of Democrats.

The last Republican who went to Washington and governed with his conservative big-boy pants on was Ronald Reagan. He largely stuck to Constitution-based policies while he unleashed unprecedented economic growth and created about 20 million new jobs.[2] He also rebuilt the armed forces and won the Cold War. Not a bad record, and from the outset he had government squarely in his crosshairs. In his first inaugural address, he made it clear that he was not part of

---

2 http://www.forbes.com/sites/peterferrara/2011/05/05/reaganomics-vs-obamanomics-facts-and-figures/.

the political establishment when he proclaimed: "Government is the problem." However, in his autobiography *An American Life*, Reagan himself admitted that despite his priority to cut government spending he came up short. "The economic recovery program was threefold: cut taxes, get government regulators out of the way, and reduce government spending. We made progress on the first two, far too little on the third."[3] So if government was too big and resistant to change in 1981, today, over three decades later, that message should be etched in marble. The fact that all of the progress made under Reagan has been eroded by the actions of career politicians—Republicans and Democrats alike—is proof of that.

It was a very harsh lesson to learn about the establishment wing of the Republican Party. Clearly it was the Progressive movement and the Democrat Party that were responsible for steering America away from our core constitutional values. It was the Republican Party, or so I thought, that was struggling to return America to those values, to take back our country. Not so much. It turns out that, rhetoric aside, the establishment wing of the Republican Party, to include most of the "*R*s" in Congress, is complicit in massive government overreach at the expense of Main Street America. In my view, establishment Republicans are just fine with big government as long as they get to be the ones in charge of it. As I write this, the 2014 midterm elections are approaching, and one of the biggest stories is that no one knows what the Republican Party stands for. They'll probably win because of the timing as well as the sheer incompetence of the Obama administration; in other words, Republicans stand to benefit not because people are voting for them so much as whom people are voting *against*. Establishment Republicans are probably just fine with that; whatever it takes to get back on top. Taking back the Senate seems to be an end unto itself for the GOP—not one syllable on what they will do if and when that happens. That's because the

---

3 Ronald Reagan, *An American Life* (New York: Threshold, 1990), 312.

Washington branch of the GOP, a.k.a. the establishment wing of the Republican Party, simply wants power—it wants to pick up the reins of government. In that aspect, they are simply Democrat-light. When you think about it, this is actually more destructive than the Democrats, who at least are willing to admit that they want a massive, all-powerful government. Republicans rail against big government, but once ensconced in Congress or the White House, the government still seems to get larger and more intrusive at the expense of Main Street America.

The result is that career politicians win, government expands, and Americans lose. We're forced to pony up ever-increasing taxes while trying to scratch out a living in a stagnant economy that is drowning under a tsunami of regulations and debt. Our representatives are addicted to spending, and we have a $17 trillion-plus national debt to show for it. Unfunded mandates, those endless entitlement commitments that our politicians have made now approaches $100 trillion. You read that right: *one hundred trillion dollars*. There isn't enough money on the planet to cover that. This stigma on America's future was not written exclusively with liberal ink. Here's the bottom line: politicians in both parties have floated our nation up poop creek and have taken away the paddles. Government, along with the professional political class behind it, *is the problem*.

If you accept the premise that the real battle is Washington vs. Main Street America, that it is government and career politicians of both political stripes who are the problem, then it quickly becomes clear that no solutions will be forthcoming from within the current political paradigm. If you are unhappy with the direction in which this country is going, then relying upon an election or a political cycle, placing your hopes in a new fresh face, switching out who runs Congress, or even the White House, *will not cure what ails us*. Under the badly bent system that now exists, our traditional political salves no longer work. Career politicians are like a cunning bacteria that has adapted to the antibiotic. They have rigged the system so that it is virtually impossible to be rid of them. They have a 10 percent approval rating but get reelected 90 percent of the time. And while they occupy DC, the federal government continues to expand, all on our dime. So at this point we must ask ourselves, what, if any, means of redress do we have?

In the army, leaders are taught that when confronted with an untenable situation in combat, in order to win they must find a way to *change the conditions on the battlefield.* That's the objective of this book, to describe why and how Main Street America must change the conditions on the *political* battlefield. I am convinced that as long as we play according to the Beltway's rules, we, the people, will continue to lose. When Main Street America finds a way to dictate terms to Washington, Main Street America will win. Fortunately for us, there is a means for doing exactly that, and it is hiding in plain sight.

Many scholars have attested to the genius, the creativity, and even the prescience with which our Founding Fathers approached the drafting of the Constitution. So it should come as little surprise that the roadmap for changing the conditions on today's political battlefield was foreseen and provided for over two centuries ago. Article V of the Constitution provides two methods for offering amendments. One way is for the Congress to do so, which is the method that has always been used. But there is another approach, one that allows the states to convene a convention wherein amendments may be proposed *without the input of Congress*. As we will see, this was a codicil insisted upon by founding father and Virginian George Mason, who sensibly maintained a healthy distrust of government. Chapter 4 will examine a convention of states in detail, but I believe that two critical amendments should emerge from such a gathering—constitutional amendments that will help reboot this nation:

- First, congressional term limits are necessary in order to rid ourselves of career politicians and the havoc they are wreaking. This book details how the country went from "citizen legislators" to career politicians, and the ramifications thereof.
- Second, a carefully crafted balanced budget amendment is necessary to hinder and reverse the growth of government and to rein in out-of-control government spending. This book explains how the rise of progressive politics and the creation of a national income tax pushed America away from our core Constitutional values and led to our present anemic situation both at home and abroad.

Both of these amendments are specifically designed to restrain and limit Congress and government, which is precisely why those same members of Congress, regardless of party, will never champion them. And that is why a Convention of States is essential to the survival of our republic. That said, it is important to acknowledge upfront that there is a great deal of controversy surrounding a Convention of States. Many, like myself, see no other alternative to a government-gone-wild. But others find cause to fear it; Chapter 4 outlines a number of their concerns.

Context is everything. That is why this book focuses on the background of how our government, designed to be limited, has become unlimited, weaponized, and oppressive. This book explains in detail how career politicians, Republican and Democrat alike, benefit from, and support an expansive government. Neither will ever self-limit. Therefore, elections, the default avenue for political change available to us, will not cure this cancer. It seems to me that this is the center of gravity behind the movement for a Convention of States. Otherwise, "stay the course and hope for the best" is our only alternative. How's that working for us?

In a nod to the late, great Warren Zevon, a quick word about my "Lawyers, Guns, and Money" approach to writing this book. In doing the research for this book, it became clear that an Article V-based Convention of States is going to get very legally nuanced, both to convene and to orchestrate. That should come as no surprise, nor should it raise any eyebrows; there is no shortage of constitutional lawyers and academicians involved in writing and debating both sides of whether or not an Article V Convention of States is viable, what amendments should be pursued, how they should be worded, and so forth. After all, America has become a very litigious place to live and work, and to succeed we will need good legal minds to suit up on our side. I'm not one of those lawyers, but I'm elbowing my way in as one of the millions of American veterans who care deeply for our republic. I mentioned earlier the oath soldiers take to support and defend the Constitution against all enemies, foreign and domestic. I can almost guarantee that if members of Congress brought the same sense of duty, honor, and selflessness that our service members bring to their profession, we would not be in this current mess. Anyway, Congress is overflowing with lawyers (by far the most common profession), and there is no shortage of constitutional scholars bouncing around either (Barack Obama, anyone?). How's that working out for us? And while many of America's Founding Fathers were lawyers and academicians, the original Constitutional Convention in Philadelphia also had its share of shopkeepers, farmers, merchants, and physicians. And soldiers. Remember this: American independence did not come out of a verdict in a court of law, nor was it written into existence at an institution of higher learning. We *won* our sovereignty on the battlefield where brave soldiers fought, bled, and died so that their countrymen could be forever free.

So this book is something of an operations order, or OPORD in military speak, not unlike how military missions are planned and executed. It explains the situation, including the all-important how and why we arrived here. It offers an honest description of the adversaries, designs a mission with specific objectives, and then details how to execute that mission. A roadmap of sorts. I think, for our purposes, that is a fitting approach. And while all of the lawyers out there are wrapping their brains around that concept, don't forget that the only reason an Article V Convention of States is available to us today is because a certain Founding Father named George Mason insisted that it be included in the Constitution. *Colonel* George Mason.

Colonel George Mason

Finally, John Adams famously said, "Facts are stubborn things." This book cites an array of facts regarding the economy, jobless numbers, debt, deficits, tax rates, regulatory costs, and many other problems, penalties, and prohibitions largely created in Washington.

They strengthen our case that government and career politicians are the problem. But it is important to remember that behind each and every one of those numbers is a frustrated, flesh and blood human being. An American who deserves much better than he or she is getting from our government. A single mom trying to make ends meet for her kids, wondering how she's going to put healthy meals on the table day after day, never mind how she is going to afford a good education for her son or daughter. An out-of-work father who seeks the dignity of a full-time job, who longs to see pride emanating out of his wife's eyes when he walks through the door after putting in an honest day's work. It is the young Millennial, brimming with hopes and dreams, shut out from starting a career, living in his or her parents' basement wondering how he or she is going to pay off a six-figure student loan, start a family, and provide a roof over their heads. Never mind how they are going to collectively deal with the federal debt and deal with government-created unfunded mandates to the tune of $100 trillion—that creeping fear that for them the American dream has become a pipe dream. Politicians and the government have lost sight of that. Instead they roll out some sleight-of-hand soaring rhetoric, waxing eloquent about "hope." That's all fine, but "hope" isn't a strategy; it's an emotion. This book is a strategy.

# CHAPTER 1

# What the Founders Unleashed and What America Has Become

Unless you're operating under a Common Core curriculum, it's pretty simple to point to the United States on a map. But discovering the real America isn't about geography. America is more of an idea that resides in our hearts and minds, one in which initiative, honesty, and hard work replaced bloodline, race, or heritage as the aristocracy of success. It was an idea that surged out of the Declaration of Independence, forcefully testing the possibility that:

> All men are created equal, that they are endowed by their Creator with certain unalienable Rights, that among these are Life, Liberty and the pursuit of Happiness.—That to secure these rights, Governments are instituted among Men, deriving their just powers from the consent of the governed,—That whenever any Form of Government becomes destructive of these ends, it is the Right of the People to alter or to abolish it, and to institute new Government.

This fresh, liberating approach, which acknowledged the need for government and defined man's relationship with it, was born out of resistance against a brutal, oppressive government that choked individual liberty and initiative. King George III's powerful and aggressive government exploited its subjects, seizing their wealth, productivity, and liberty in order to sustain and expand. American Colonists finally struck back against that oppression, ultimately winning their independence and launching a new nation. I call it the First American Wave. The founders set about creating an entirely new form of government, one limited in scope that would empower individuals and enable free markets. "Liberty under law" was an ingenious system in that it meshed with man's innate incentive-driven tendencies and self-betterment. It was new algebra that created a unique American equation that embodied life, liberty, and the pursuit of happiness.

> **The American equation:** limited government + free markets x individual liberty = prosperity

That new math offered a paradigm whereby anyone willing to work could achieve a level of success that previously was only attainable by kings and conquerors through oppression and conquest. As Dinesh D'Sousa pointed out in his January 30, 2014, debate with American terrorist William Aires at Dartmouth University, the beauty of America was that this new system enabled "the greatest invention of all; the invention of wealth creation." [4] Now people could achieve wealth without taking it from someone else. The result? Never in human history have so many advancements and improvements come to fruition so quickly and efficiently. In a very short period of time, American entrepreneurs changed the world by creating unprecedented opportunity and wealth, which lifted millions out of poverty. Life spans dramatically increased through advances in medicine, health care, and education. American ingenuity and wealth left footprints on the moon, explored the far reaches of the solar system, and probed the depths of the oceans. It brought together a global power projection with a sense of doing the right thing that

[4] http://live.dineshdsouza.com.

liberated millions of people from tyranny around the world. It made America the world's indispensable nation.

As novel and as empowering as this was for most, America was not created in perfection. The notion that "all men" were created equal had to ring pretty hollow for the millions of black slaves in the southern states. While most of the founders were antislavery, had they attempted to constitutionally outlaw that practice at the outset, the slave-holding southern states would have walked, and America would have never coalesced. In order for the Constitution to be ratified and the American experiment to move forward, the founders hit upon a "Three-Fifths Compromise" to count slaves for representational purposes. Today, revisionists and America haters point to the Three-Fifths Compromise as evidence that the Constitution, and by extension this country, is inherently racist. In fact the opposite is true; the Three-Fifths Compromise was a tactic to limit the congressional representation of the slave-holding states. Moreover, the original Constitution did not contain the words "race," "slavery," "slave," "white," "black," or any other term that would lead anyone with two brain cells to rub together to believe that America's founding document was racist.

It would, however, take another bloody war to right these wrongs. The Civil War ripped our nation apart, amassing a far higher body count than all the nation's other wars - combined. It came at a very high price, but the last full measure given by hundreds of thousands of young men brought about the end of slavery in America and put "paid" to the notion that *all* men truly are created equal. It resulted in the Thirteenth, Fourteenth, and Fifteenth Amendments to the Constitution. Call it the Second American Wave. One direct and powerful outcome of that Second American Wave, and the high price we paid for it, is that in 2008 Americans, both black and white, elected an African American as their president.

## The Collapse of the American Dream and American Exceptionalism

America is the result of an agreement of sorts between the founders and the citizenry. It is what Ben Franklin meant back in 1787 when, in response to Mrs. Powel's query of "Well Doctor, what have we got, a republic or a monarchy?" he said, "A republic, *if you can keep it*." They set it up and placed it in our hands; it falls to us to maintain it, to nurture it, and to protect it. Keeping it means adhering to America's unique "owner's manual," our Constitution. It means perpetuating limited government, free markets, and individual liberty. Clearly, Dr. Franklin was skeptical from the get-go. Everyone said he was a very wise man.

And sure enough, today, by almost any metric you want to apply, the energy behind American Exceptionalism is rapidly dissipating, and the promise behind the American dream is being rolled back. What is happening? Why are our brilliant and unique pastels fading away? The answer is obvious—the federal government, designed to be limited, has become virtually limitless. Because of that, our individual liberty, meant to be expansive, is being choked out. The federal government has distended into a colossal, relentless parasite that is devouring our wealth and productivity, constraining our opportunity, and destroying our initiative. All in order to sustain and expand itself.

How did this happen? How did a modest annual government operating budget of around 2 percent of GDP (wars notwithstanding) swell to 25 percent of GDP? In 2014 the federal government fleeced us for a mind numbing $3 trillion in taxes, but even with that largess they did not come close to covering expenditures of about $3.5 trillion, more deficits to pile on top of the existing $17 trillion of federal debt. How did a national psyche forged upon bright-eyed initiative and rugged individualism devolve into "food stamp nation" where, according to a 2013 CATO Institute study, "The current welfare system provides such a high level of benefits that it acts as a disincentive for work."[5] It is no wonder that in 2014 some 110 million healthy and capable American citizens, about half of the workforce, just said screw it and choose not to work at all. Why work when you can get paid more sitting at home? We're being encouraged to rely not upon ourselves to thrive, but upon government to survive. That may pass for "social justice" in today's victim-laden vocabulary, but it sure isn't American.

How is it that our original boutique government, a humble affair of exactly three departments (War, State, and Treasury), grew into a multimillion-strong army of bureaucrats spread across untold numbers of departments, agencies, offices, bureaus, annexes, and programs? Why does this expansive government require a domestic force of over 120,000 heavily armed agents who work in so-called "regulatory" agencies such as the IRS and the EPA with both the capability and authority to intimidate American citizens and compel compliance? Why is the most vibrant form of free market capitalism in history morphing into a Washington-centric system of crony capitalism where government and career politicians get to pick winners and losers in the private sector in exchange for campaign contributions and political support? Why did our "citizen legislators" in congress turn into an isolated class of career politicians who benefit from a powerful, expansive government? Why is our government robbing Millenials and future generations of their American birthright? Most important, what the hell can we do about it? That is the purpose of this book—to explore these questions and to offer a way out. It describes the concurrent rise of liberal, progressive politics that worships at the altar of big government, and how this in turn gave rise to an elite professional political class in Washington.

---

5 http://www.cato.org/publications/white-paper/work-versus-welfare-trade.

Thomas Jefferson knew the answer to all of these questions well over two hundred years ago when he said, "My reading of history convinces me that most bad government results from too much government." Too much government. For Mr. Jefferson, the founder of the Democrat Party, the ramifications of heavy-handed government were up close and personal. Sadly as happens all too often, history repeats. By today's Democrat Party standards, Thomas Jefferson would be dismissed as a wild-eyed Tea Party radical. So while the dates and circumstances differ, the outcome is virtually the same; today we are again suffocating from too much government However there is one huge difference between now and then. Unlike the second half of the eighteenth century, today we have a Constitution, a national owners' manual to follow. The problem is that our professional politicians feel neither obligated nor compelled to do so; limited government and personal liberty may be good for Main Street America, but it does nothing to facilitate gaining and holding power inside the Beltway.

**The Mediocre States of America**

No government in history has ever spent itself rich, and the United States of America will be no exception. Regardless of what they promise, this destructive path of ever-expanding government at the behest of an elite class of professional politicians will not, cannot, lead America back to prosperity. America is quickly sliding into becoming an also-ran, a tepid state of mediocrity where the American dream is relegated to the history books. We'll be telling our kids and grandkids what it was like to live in America when she was exceptional. Unfortunately our kids and grandkids aren't going to be very happy hearing those stories given that they're the ones who will get to deal with Himalayan debt, FDR-like tax rates, crumbling infrastructure in a second-rate economy hamstrung by reams of regulations. Instead of focusing on buying a home, saving some cash, and putting their kids through school, they're going to have to figure out how to pay for some $100 trillion in government entitlement promises. Because if they don't people are going to get angry (more on that below). It will be the first time in American history when a future generation of Americans actually had *less* opportunity than their parents. Moreover, the Mediocre States of America will gradually become incapable of the most fundamental responsibility found in the preamble to the Constitution—to "provide for the common defense," much less any ability to oppose the bad actors of the world. Nature might abhor a vacuum, but the bad actors in the world thrive on it. Iran, al Qaeda, ISIS, Hamas, expansionist-minded Vladimir Putin in Russia, Syrian butcher Bashar Assad, Boco Harum in Nigeria, the unhinged and nuclear-armed whack jobs in North Korea, the morbidly powerful drug cartels operating with impunity on our southern borders, they all *love* a vacuum. When the deterrent that is the USA goes AWOL, the killers come out to play. Global stability and security is weakened, American national interests are threatened, and our allies, particularly Israel, face existential threats. Sadly this is already happening now, and their horrific acts will only gain momentum.

As worrisome as that all is, an insolvent America is going to get much, much worse right here at home. Career politicians in Washington have recklessly overpromised and overcommitted to spending other people's money (our money) in order to remain popular and to stay in office. Earlier I cited the massive size of the so-called unfunded mandates to the tune of $100 trillion. That amounts to the fiscal commitments that our politicians have made in the form of entitlements—Social Security, Medicare, Medicaid, and Obamacare. On top of that, the government also pays billions more in government employee pensions, veterans benefits, and medical care for both. There is also an annual expenditure of about $1 trillion in welfare payments. Then, of course, there is a throbbing federal debt over $17 trillion, which grows every day, every hour, every minute.

## Next Stop: Detroit

If we war-game out where all of this is going, it gets as ugly as it is inevitable. What's going to happen on the streets across the USA when those 110 million Americans who rely upon the government for their existence are told that their Supplemental Nutrition Assistance Program (SNAP) cards (the twenty-first century version of food stamps) will no longer be refilled, cash-assistance programs are broke, the millions of Obamaphones don't have any more minutes, the other "freebies" meds, healthcare, vocational training, social services, utility assistance, housing, childcare, etc., that come under the laundry list of ninety-some means-tested "free" welfare programs out there. What happens when the government reneges on those commitments?

What's going to happen when Social Security and Medicare recipients, the millions of veterans and retired government workers with pensions and healthcare are all told that from here out they will only be getting pennies on the dollar, if that? As the $100 trillion in unfunded mandates stops being an unfathomable number on a piece of paper and starts to become reality, impacting the lives of over half of our population, how are people going to react? And since there are very few jobs to be had, most Americans who have become dependent upon the government won't be able to find a source of legal income. And to put a cherry on top, when the Federal Reserve cranks up the printing presses and expands the money supply to try and pay the bills, hyperinflation will send costs soaring. A gallon of gas could go to $100, a loaf of bread $50, a pound of butter $75. What is going to play out on the streets of America then?

The government has spent the last century stripping away the virtues of initiative and individual responsibility in order to create a dependency upon this nanny state. But as Margaret Thatcher shrewdly observed, "The problem with Socialism is that you eventually run out of others people's money." Our career politicians have vastly, recklessly overpromised. When, not if, our government starts to renege on its promises and commitments, America will descend quickly from an ordered society into massive civil unrest, riots in the streets, and violent anarchy. That may seem farfetched here in America. These things do happen, but always somewhere else, right? But could anarchy actually happen in America? Sure. In fact it already has in some places; think New Orleans after Hurricane Katrina. All it took was for the fabric of law and order to disappear against the backdrop of a natural disaster, and suddenly everyone got medieval. Even a better example for our purposes is Detroit, a once-proud city that also suffered a disaster. Except that Detroit's catastrophe didn't come from Mother Nature; it was a man-made government tsunami.

Detroit, Michigan, was once one of the wealthiest, most beautiful cities in the entire world. In 1960 Detroit boasted the highest per capita standard of living of any city in America; it was a laboratory for what is possible when the private sector is unleashed. Thanks to a market-driven auto industry, jobs and opportunities were plentiful, and people thrived upon living in a modern, safe city. Fast forward to 2013, when Detroit became the biggest city in American history to file for bankruptcy proceedings. What once was a cultural magnet is now largely a burnt-out slum, overrun by crime and squalor. Everyone with the means to do so has long since fled to the 'burbs. Nature is reclaiming great swaths of what used to be beautiful neighborhoods, buildings, parks, and schools. Ramshackle houses sell for $20. The Detroit Police Department has publicly warned tourists not to come to the city, and has also advised citizens to arm themselves. Public services are problematic at best; average response time to a 911 call in Detroit is one hour, if the police show up at all. Were Hollywood producer John Carpenter to film a Midwestern-based sequel to his post-Apocalyptic movies *Escape from New York* and *Escape from L.A.*, Detroit would make a perfect real-life set.

How in the world did this happen? It is the direct result of a meddling progressive government, rife with crony capitalism and politicians picking winners and losers, rewarding themselves and aligning with labor unions to punish the private sector, all under the guise of "social justice" and equal outcome.

The American auto industry, the goose that laid the golden egg in Detroit, was dealt a huge blow. Today America still has a thriving auto industry, but it is now largely located in southern right-to-work states where BMW, Nissan, Toyota, and numerous other car manufacturers have set up plants, employ tens of thousands of workers, and produce an excellent product. But Detroit also represents something else: it is an all-too-real case study of what awaits the rest of the country unless we do something now. What's the worst part of this dilemma? Just like Detroit, what is happening in Washington is a self-inflicted wound, courtesy of big government and career politicians. Somebody cue Snake Plissken.

By the way, the longest serving Member of congress is John Dingell, whose District includes Detroit. He's been in congress since Eisenhower was president and General Motors was cranking out those awesome 1955 Chevys. Dingell literally presided over the downfall of Detroit, watching it dissolve from beauty into beast. But hey, at least he came out ok, Dingell personally become a multimillionaire in the process and his wife just took over his congressional seat, the same one he inherited from his father. How's that working out for Detroit? More on Dingell and his ilk in Chapter 2 when we examine career politicians.

## America's Third Wave Is Coming

This will be the Third American Wave, and like the first two American waves—the first that was our founding, the second that eradicated slavery—it is going to be a tsunami. And also like the other two, the outcome is uncertain. We won the American Revolution and the Civil War, but then as now, outcomes aren't guaranteed.

So the most important question is how can America win this fight and get back on the right track? How to remedy this problem, pacing Mr. Jefferson, of too much government? What can be done to curb the out-of-control spending, stop an ever-expanding government, return liberty to individual Americans, and evict the career politicians who created and perpetuate this debacle? How can we get out in front of this coming wave and turn it to our advantage?

Unlike America's First and Second Waves, today we have a huge advantage in that we already have a roadmap to victory, laid out in the American owners' manual, aka the Constitution. We must find our way back to those core constitutional principles of limited government, individual liberty, and free markets that fueled the American dream and American Exceptionalism in the first place. Two constitutional amendments would go a long way to making America well again. A balanced budget amendment would force the federal government to operate under a balanced budget and live within its means so that we could stop this out-of-control spending and begin the task of reducing our debt and shrinking government. Also, if we could enact congressional term limits, we could rid ourselves of an insulated professional political class that thrives on crony capitalism and an expansive, all-powerful government (yes I'm talking about Republicans too, as you will see later on). The Constitution provides the way ahead for this, and the route necessarily circumvents Washington.

## Article V of the Constitution

Now, per Article V of the Constitution, there are exactly two ways to proffer constitutional amendments. One way is how it has always been done, which is for Congress to do so. Clearly this would be the most straightforward and expedient way, but I think we all agree that wherever three or more politicians are gathered, self-limits aren't going to be in the lexicon. Moreover, politicians in Washington have the power and the authority to voluntarily do what constitutional amendments would force them to do. They could stop their out-of-control spending, shrink the government, and rein in the federal government regulatory agencies (a.k.a. Power Ministries) that target citizens and small businesses. Members of Congress could easily impose term limits upon themselves, and stop the exercise of "pay-to-play" crony capitalism and of putting party over country. They could stop meting out trillions of taxpayer dollars to companies and organizations in return for kickbacks by way of campaign contributions and political support that keeps them in power. They could find the courage to enact entitlement reform, given the dire fiscal situation we are in and that they themselves created. They could reform the tax code, dump the IRS, allow state and local governments to determine their own education needs, and roll back the deluge of federal regulations that plague the private sector and that cost Americans trillions of dollars every year. But they won't; governments and politicians don't give up power that easily, regardless of which political party is calling the shots. The professional political class of both political parties will whip this big government horse until it drops, pointing fingers at each other all the way down. They will never self-limit. Change will only come from outside of the Beltway, which brings us to the second method of proposing constitutional amendments, and that is through a convention of states. Chapter 4 will explain this in much more detail, but for now, here are the broad brush strokes: Article V of the Constitution provides a mechanism to offer constitutional amendments coming out of a convention called by two-thirds of the state legislatures. That means that thirty-four states, working together, may propose amendments to the Constitution *with neither the participation nor the approval of the federal government or the US Congress.*

**Last Resort?**

If this solution sort of has a "last resort" feel to it, well that's just about where we are. That's because nothing else within the current American political process can or will break through the phalanx of big government and career politicians that are poisoning our system. Elections no longer matter, at least not nearly to the extent that those running for office would have us believe. As we'll see in chapter 2, congressional elections are largely precooked. Additionally, flipping which party controls what chamber in Congress, or the White House, will not deter this juggernaut, as chapter 3 will explain. A political cycle or two, a new political strategy, recycled messaging, or the next new political savior, are all largely irrelevant under the current paradigm. If you doubt that, ask yourself where all of the progress made under the Reagan years has gone. The massive expansion of the economy, tens of millions of jobs created, thriving new businesses, a victory over Communism in the Cold War, and building the strongest military force in the history of the world, most of that has either vanished or is inertial. The same goes for the progress during the Clinton administration, when the president and Speaker Gingrich worked together to "end welfare as we know it," and to eradicate the federal debt. With fifty million Americans on food stamps, almost one hundred million out of the workforce, and a debt of $17+ trillion, all of that pragmatic progress has been erased, and then some.

It is also important to acknowledge that a huge part of the problem resides squarely with an American public that chooses to ignore what is going on in their government. Many people are (understandably) disgusted by the political process. Others are too busy admiring Miley Cyrus's twerking prowess or they are just all a-tingle about ongoing drama being played out in the Real Housewives of Dubuque. Whatever the reason, most Americans can't or don't recognize the steady government-caused erosion of the nation, and my sense is that Washington is just fine with that.

There remains a minority of stalwart, well-meaning citizens who dutifully participate in the political process. They follow the issues, support their candidates, volunteer to knock doors, phone bank, work the polls, and vote. They are doing what they can to effect change within the confines of our current political system. And most of them are pretty frustrated. If you're reading this, you're probably one of them. Are you happy with the direction of your country? Are you willing to do something about it?

## Changing the Conditions on the Battlefield

Much of combat involves dealing with the unexpected, such as occasions when military leaders find themselves in an untenable situation on the battlefield. On July 2, 1863, Union Colonel Joshua Chamberlain was perched up on Little Round Top during the battle of Gettysburg. His Twentieth Maine Regiment, tasked with defending the important far left flank of the Union line, was shot to pieces, out of ammunition, and about to be overrun by Confederate forces. What to do? He could have obeyed orders and died in place, hoping they could hold out long enough to make a difference before being overrun. Instead Chamberlain did what was least expected, not only by the enemy, but even by his own troops; he ordered his men to fix bayonets and charge straight into the advancing Rebel forces. The Twentieth Maine surprised those Alabama troops, won the battle in a rout and held the all-important Union left flank. Chamberlain was successful because he eschewed standard operating procedures and did the unexpected. Faced with an untenable situation, he changed the conditions on the battlefield to his advantage. Now that's easier said than done, and history is replete with gory examples of battles where military commanders followed orders, did what was expected and lost. Had Chamberlain stayed in place and been overrun, history wouldn't condemn him for losing. Nor would we know who he was. Moreover, had the Union lost at Gettysburg, the outcome of the Civil War and the fate of the United States of America could have been very different.

I'd argue that similar principles apply to the battlefield of politics and to the quandary now facing America. There are no viable solutions for Main Street America within the current political paradigm. As long as we keep relying upon our elected representatives and the government to act in our collective self-interests, Main Street America will continue to be overrun. Until we decide to take away the career politicians' ability to permanently park their butts in Washington and to spend our money without limits, we will continue to lose. So it is up to us, Main Street Americans, to change the conditions on the political battlefield to our advantage. The purpose of this book is to explain the reasons behind our dilemma, articulate a solution, and offer the means to enact that solution. It falls to this generation of Americans to bring about a constitutional reset that will begin to restore America's core values of limited government, individual liberty, and free markets. Because our shortfalls do not come from, as Washington would have us believe, an excess of liberty. Rather, America's shortfalls come from an excess of government. Fortunately for us, we don't have to guess as to the right solution; our dilemma was foreseen and provided for over two centuries ago by the drafters of our Constitution. So if an Article V Convention of States seems like a difficult path, it also comes with the blessing, the wisdom, and the optimism of America's Founding Fathers. Here's the bottom line:

# CHAPTER 2

# The Problem with Career Politicians

Old Ben Franklin liked to say, "Guests, like fish, begin to smell after three days." If he were around today, he'd probably come up with a similar adage for the career politicians who take up permanent residence in Washington. It hasn't always been thus. Once upon a time, we had "citizen legislators" who put their real lives on hold in order to serve in Congress for a limited time, and for minimal remuneration. After one or two terms, they would return to their real lives to live under the laws that they had passed. It was a means to an end, selfless duty in service of country that one would step forward to perform. But things have changed quite a bit in the ornate halls and plush offices of Congress. Selfless service is now a self-serving end unto itself. In a life imitates art moment, Jimmy Stewart's role as the high-minded, homespun senator in *Mr. Smith Goes to Washington* has mutated into Kevin Spacey's manipulative, power-hungry Congressman Frank Underwood in the television series *House of Cards*. Being a member of Congress today is a lucrative end unto itself—a lofty position of power, perks, benefits, and attention. It is also frequently a means to attain personal wealth through crony capitalism and at taxpayer expense.

## Friends and Family Approval Rating

Congressional public approval ratings usually clock in at or under 10 percent. Think of it as a "friends and family" plan for a mobile phone provider; the only people in America who don't despise Congress are their friends and family. Yet somehow those same reviled incumbents manage to get themselves reelected again and again and again, cycle after election cycle, at a rate of around 90 percent.[6] The so-called "bloodletting" midterm elections of 2010, when the mantra across the country was "throw them all out," returned 85 percent of incumbents. In his article entitled "EXography: Americans revile Congress—but keep re-electing incumbents over and over" *Washington Examiner* reporter Luke Rosiak offers some excellent insight into the permanent politician phenomenon. For example, in 1912, a scant twenty-six members of Congress had been in office for twenty years; only four of those had hung around for thirty years. Fast forward one hundred years to 2012, we find that 147 lawmakers have been in office for twenty years, and fifty-three have been fixtures for thirty or more years.[7]

Moreover, a Congressional Research Service (CRS) study conducted in 2013 revealed a steady increase in the tenure of members of Congress in the twentieth century, largely coinciding with the events described above. For most of the nineteenth century, anywhere from 30 to 60 percent of congressmen did not bother to seek reelection at all. In fact many departed before their term was even up. Fast forward

---

6 http://www.outsidethebeltway.com/house-and-senate-incumbent-re-election-rates-top-90/.

7 Luke Rosiak, EXography: Americans Revile Congress-but Keep re-electing incumbents over and over *Washington Examiner,* August 14, 2014. http://www.washingtonexaminer.com/exography-americans-revile-congress-but-keep-re-electing-incumbents/article/2552000.

to the twenty-first century and the average for politicians who do not seek reelection is a miniscule 11 percent.[8] So what happened?

How did citizen legislators who served a term or two out of a sense of duty for minimal compensation turn into an untouchable class of career politicians who spend decades in Washington earning annual salaries, perks, and benefits in the millions of dollars, and who default to expanding government as a solution to every problem? Or how is it that, as Rosiak points out, Congress scores lower than cockroaches in public opinion polls, but the vermin are easier to get rid of? Not surprisingly, our professional political class is an offshoot of the progressive political movement in America.

## The Rise of Progressivism in America

Those who ignore history are bound to repeat it, so it is important to take a brief look at how and why the United States went off of our constitutional rails. In the late nineteenth century, a new, "progressive" political movement began to gain favor in America. Among other things, progressives were bent on curing societal problems as they saw them; you know, national malware such as social justice and economic equality. In other words, they apparently interpreted the Declaration of Independence to read "life, liberty and the *guarantee* of happiness." Progressives posited that the levers of government, when expanded and manipulated by the right sort of people (i.e., them) could be the champion of justice and righter of all wrongs and would make everybody equal and happy—a heroic government wearing a cape, from which all blessings would flow. "But what about the Constitution and limited government," some people asked. Redundant. Outdated. In the way.

8 Matthew Eric Glassman, Congressional Careers: Service Tenure and Patterns of Member Service, 1789-2015. *Congressional Research Service*, January 3, 2015, p5. https://www.fas.org/sgp/crs/misc/R41545.pdf

America started the twentieth century with a presidential assassination that thrust a young, hard-charging progressive Republican into the White House. Theodore Roosevelt reveled in the exercise of power. His inherent understanding of the importance of a strong navy, and the financial and industrial base necessary to expand it, coupled with a willingness to protect American interests and citizens wherever they were found propelled the United States into a global power to be reckoned with. Many saw the powerful young nation as embodied in its vigorous youthful president. Domestically Roosevelt set about turbocharging government in his own robust, larger-than-life image. An energetic populist, perhaps the first chief executive to understand and utilize the power of the press to further his goals and ambitions, Roosevelt also set many precedents in expanding federal oversight and regulations and arguably created the precedent for the modern bureaucratic/ administrative state. In his unsuccessful Bull Moose campaign for president in 1912, Roosevelt espoused a "New Nationalism" that was decidedly progressive. However progressivism as a model of governance, combined with the constitutional and fiscal means necessary to exercise it, came to fruition under the hand of a quiet academic named Woodrow.

Woodrow Wilson had built a distinguished academic career out of studying and writing about government. An examination of his writings and speeches as he grew in prominence gives a clear indication where the twenty-eighth president of the United States wanted to steer the nation. As Ronald J. Pestritto explains in his book *Woodrow Wilson and the Roots of Modern Liberalism*, the founders believed that human nature would never change, governments must therefore be structured accordingly. Wilson stridently disagreed, believing these views to be "anti-Progressive."[9] For Wilson, the separation of powers, and all of the other institutional remedies that

[9] Ronald J. Pestritto, *Woodrow Wilson and the Roots of Modern Liberalism* (New York: Rowman & Littlefield, 2005), 5.

the founders employed against the danger of faction, stood in the way of government's exercising its power in accord with the dictates of progress.[10] Moreover, placing limits upon government did nothing to protect personal liberty; it was nothing more than "a prescription for choking the life out of our governing institutions."[11] That sounds very much as if Wilson had it exactly wrong, that the citizenry existed to benefit government, not the other way around.

In other words, the Constitution was a relic that was getting in the way of expanding government and telling people how to live. As Pestritto explains, Jeffersonian limited government may have constituted the *history* of liberty in America, but it played no part in Wilson's vision of America's future.[12] This was the genesis of progressive governance in America, which one century later has ripened into the European-style social welfare state that it is today. I recommend reading Pestritto's book; it will forever alter your view of American political history.

## The Sixteenth Amendment: Funding Progressive Utopia

Espousing the virtues of progressive big government was one thing, but that in itself wasn't enough to make it happen. This transformation was going to take a lot of money; there was no way that Wilson and team would be able to expand government on a meager fiscal diet of tariffs and excise taxes. But as 1913 rolled around and Wilson took over the White House, the Sixteenth Amendment legalizing a federal income tax was ratified and took effect. The founders had been against direct taxation of the citizenry unless the funds raised were apportioned to each state according to population (Article 1, Section 9). Heretofore, the federal government ran on tariffs, and property

10 Pestritto, *Woodrow Wilson*, 6.
11 Pestritto, *Woodrow Wilson*, 119.
12 Pestritto, *Woodrow Wilson* 256.

and excise taxes. But on February 3, 1913, all of that changed with the Sixteenth Amendment:

> The Congress shall have power to lay and collect taxes on incomes, from whatever source derived, without apportionment among the several states, and without regard to any census or enumeration.

Those thirty words have had a profound impact on the trajectory of this nation. Prior to that, annual federal government expenditures were 2 to 4 percent of national GDP, war-related spikes notwithstanding. That's quite a contrast with current annual government spending running as high as 25 percent of GDP, or almost $4 trillion a year, according to *usgovernmentspending.com*. (Warning: don't visit that website without a stiff drink within arm's reach.) With revenue coming in, the bureaucracy could be expanded, new government departments and agencies created, and bureaucrats hired. Progressive social justice and income equality were surely just around the corner.

The Sixteenth Amendment opened the income tax spigot and turned the federal government into the world's biggest ATM machine. It also turned the collective heads of congressional officeholders

**Tax Freedom Day**

TaxFoundation.org calculates "Tax Freedom Day," which is the day when American taxpayers have finally worked enough to pay off the tax bill. For 2014, Americans spent 111 days working for Uncle Sam.[13] Subtract weekends and holidays and we come up with about 250 workdays per year. So if you're a full-time employee, about 44 percent of your work life doesn't accrue to your income; it goes to the government. Americans pay more in taxes than they spend on food and housing combined, but the career politicians tell us we still aren't paying our "fair share."

13 "Tax Freedom Day," http://taxfoundation.org/tax-topics/tax-freedom-day.

and office seekers. "Follow the money" is usually the best way to get to the truth, and all those taxpayer dollars pouring into Washington certainly changed how politicians viewed their role and their reason for being there. After all, per the Constitution, Congress held the purse strings, and thanks to the new tax on income, the purse was starting to get heavy indeed. So a seat in Congress took on a new, powerful, lucrative sheen, an end unto itself, a career. Thus it isn't surprising that following closely on the heels of the Sixteenth Amendment, some structural changes were made that directly impacted Congress, changes that helped strengthen incumbents' hold on their office: the Seventeenth Amendment and the Apportionment Act.

### The Seventeenth Amendment: Job Security for Senators

Written into the DNA of America's founding was the delegation of authority down and away from federal government, toward states and individuals. This was explicit in a number of ways, including the Tenth Amendment:

> The powers not delegated to the United States by the Constitution, nor prohibited by it to the States, are reserved to the States respectively, or to the people.

*Federalist Papers* nos. 52 to 66, which largely focus on the composition of the legislative branch, provide a historical tour of a wide range of legislative bodies throughout history: the Tribunes in Rome, Sparta's Ephori, the Cosmi in Crete, the reforms of Solon in Athens, the Senate in Carthage, Britain's House of Commons and Lords, even the constitutions of selected American Colonies. Clearly the founders did their due diligence in researching what would become the United States Congress, including how to carefully balance power both horizontally between big and small states as well as vertically between the states and federal government:

> Among the various modes which might have been devised for constituting this branch of the government, that which has been proposed by the convention is probably the most congenial with the public opinion. It is recommended by the double advantage of favoring a select appointment, and of giving to the State governments such an agency in the formation of the federal government as must secure the authority of the former [State governments], and may form a convenient link between the two systems.—*Federalist* 62

And:

> The Senate … will derive its powers from the States, as political and coequal societies; and these will be represented on the principle of equality in the Senate, as they now are in the existing Congress. —*Federalist* 39

Thus Article I, Section 3.1 of the Constitution:

> The Senate of the United States shall be composed of two Senators from each State, chosen by the Legislature thereof, for six Years; and each Senator shall have one Vote.

By contrast, House members were meant to be closer to the people:

> The House of Representatives will derive its powers from the people of America; and the people will be represented in the same proportion, and on the same principle, as they are in the legislature of a particular State.—*Federalist* 39.

Thus Article I, Section 2.1 of the Constitution:

> The House of Representatives shall be composed of Members chosen every second Year by the People of the several States, and the Electors in each State shall have the Qualifications requisite for Electors of the most numerous Branch of the State Legislature.

That the lower chamber of Congress would be elected by popular vote and the upper chamber by the legislators of each state was by design. It was a deliberate balancing act that placed the Senate above what would likely be emotionally driven legislation coming out of the popularly elected House. At the same time, because state governments reside nearest to their constituencies and understand the respective needs and concerns at the local level, empowering those local legislators to choose their senators ensured that the upper chamber of Congress would better understand and represent the disparate concerns of each state.

However in the late nineteenth and early twentieth centuries, numerous charges of bribery and corruption were leveled at numerous states, as well as occasional legislative deadlocks surrounding the choice of senators. Progressive politicians pointed to these instances as reasons for switching to a popular vote for senators. Progressives also understood very well that severing state oversight of who served in the US Senate would dramatically strengthen the federal government. Woodrow Wilson was a strong advocate, and well-known progressive Democrat William Jennings Bryan successfully led the charge. On April 8, 1913, the Seventeenth Amendment was ratified.

> The Senate of the United States shall be composed of two Senators from each State, elected by the people thereof, for six years; and each Senator shall have one vote. The electors

> in each State shall have the qualifications requisite for electors of the most numerous branch of the State legislatures.
>
> When vacancies happen in the representation of any State in the Senate, the executive authority of such State shall issue writs of election to fill such vacancies: Provided, That the legislature of any State may empower the executive thereof to make temporary appointments until the people fill the vacancies by election as the legislature may direct.
>
> This amendment shall not be so construed as to affect the election or term of any Senator chosen before it becomes valid as part of the Constitution.

In addition to strengthening the federal government at the expense of the states, it altered the landscape in the Senate. Senators no longer needed to kowtow to their respective states; party loyalty in Washington was more relevant. And with piles of taxpayer dollars now coming in, Congress held the purse strings, and that purse was getting heavily laden with taxpayer coinage, and being a member of Congress was becoming a lucrative means unto itself. The negative impact this amendment has had on our nation has been substantial. It also hasn't done anything for senators representing their state; a great indicator of this is that today many US senators no longer even bother to live in the states they supposedly represent. They maintain a placeholder address, but they live full time in Washington.

Ask yourself these questions: if senators were still chosen by State legislators, do you think that our federal debt would be the staggering $17 trillion-plus that it is now, or would federal spending be much closer to intake? Would federal taxes be higher or lower? Would the federal government be churning out regulations and mandates that cost states and individuals trillions of dollars per year? Would there be a Department of Education imposing massive dictates such No Child Left Behind or Common Core? Federal school lunch mandates? Would there be a Dodd-Frank bill, a fifteen-thousand-page monstrosity of rules and regulations that raises costs that has an undue impact on smaller local banks? Would there be Obamacare?

**Case Study: The Seventeenth Amendment and Obamacare**

The Affordable Care Act (ACA), a.k.a. Obamacare, is the latest in a litany of federal entitlements that overpromise, underperform, and will hasten America's bankruptcy. I believe this law is the result of the ramifications of the Seventeenth Amendment. Obamacare passed by only one vote in the Senate on a strict party line vote. Democrat senators supported it under immense pressure from the Obama White House and the Democrat Party despite virulent public opposition to Obamacare in a majority of states. In fact twenty-seven states actually sued the federal government on the grounds that the ACA was unconstitutional. However, all eighteen Democrat senators who represented those states voted in favor of Obamacare.

States suing the federal government over Obamacare (including the number of Democrat senators at the time):

Alabama, Alaska (1), Arizona, Colorado (2), Florida (1), Georgia, Idaho, Indiana, Kansas, Louisiana (1), Maine, Michigan (2), Mississippi, Nebraska (1), Nevada (1), North Dakota (1), Oklahoma, Ohio (1), Pennsylvania (1), South Carolina, South Dakota (1), Texas, Utah, Virginia (2), Washington (2), Wisconsin (1), Wyoming

In Virginia, there was aggressive vocal opposition to the ACA, including in the capitol of Richmond, where then Virginia Attorney General Ken Cuccinelli filed an early lawsuit. Despite this, both of Virginia's Democrat senators, Mark Warner and Jim Webb, voted in favor of Obamacare. Elsewhere the White House resorted to naked bribery, offering hundreds of millions of taxpayer dollars by way of pork projects to persuade any Democrat senator who displayed a modicum of loyalty to his or her respective state. In Louisiana, one of the twenty-seven states suing the federal government, Democrat Senator Mary Landreu was bought off with the $300 million "Louisiana Purchase." Senator Ben Nelson from Nebraska (lawsuit against Obamacare) benefitted from the $100 million "Cornhusker Kickback," and Senator Bill Nelson from Florida (lawsuit against Obamacare) sold out for "Gatorade." So where was their loyalty? Were they loyal to their respective states that were suing the federal government over Obamacare and the citizens therein? Hardly. In every case party loyalty trumped the clear will of their constituents as well as that of their state governments. And that's why we have Obamacare, the biggest entitlement of them all.

### The Apportionment Act: Job Security for Representatives

While the Seventeenth Amendment helps protect career politicians in the Senate, the Apportionment Act has a similar effect in the House of Representatives. The Apportionment Act, which also went into effect in 1913, capped the House of Representatives at 435 members. At that time the population of the United States was about ninety-two million, which meant that each House member represented roughly 211,000 citizens. Today the US population is about 317 million, which means that members of the House now represent almost 730,000 people. Absent the Apportionment Act, there would now be approximately fifteen hundred politicians in the House of Representatives.[14] If you agree that government is the problem, then having fifteen hundred politicians in the House of Representatives probably sounds like a really bad horror movie. But

---

14 "The Super-Sized Congress," *Rational World*, April 23, 2012, http://rationalworldblog.wordpress.com/2012/04/23/the-super-sized-congress/.

the reality is that the bigger the congressional district, the greater the power and influence of each representative. The bigger the congressional district, the more difficult it becomes for a challenger to wage a viable campaign, and therefore the higher the probability of reelection for the incumbent. That power and influence translates to ease of reelection and an ironclad incumbency, which in turn means bigger government, more spending, more regulations for them and less individual liberty for you and me. The organization Ballotopedia projected that for the 2014 midterm elections, only about twenty-nine of the 435 House races will actually be competitive.[15] That's only about 6 percent; the other 94 percent of House seats are a done deal, decided before the polls even open. Despite this, hundreds of millions of dollars will be spent on campaigns. The popular sound bite that "elections have consequences" used by politicians to motivate voters may sound good, but the reality in the vast majority of cases is that the outcome has already been precooked. Baseball fans will forever remember the 1919 World Series and the infamous Chicago "Black Sox" where the series outcome was bought and paid for before the first pitch was thrown. Or the first vote cast.

**Gerrymandering**

Gerrymander: *verb* to manipulate the boundaries of (an electoral constituency) so as to favor one party or class.

The practice of gerrymandering serves to further insulate members of the House of Representatives from challenge and accountability. While methods vary from state to state, it is decidedly a political process whereby congressional districts are drawn to reflect party demographics of the incumbent. Gerrymandering is a bipartisan

15 "Incorrect Projections Cause Campaign Costs to Skyrocket," *Lucy Burns Institute*, November 13, 2013, http://www.lucyburns.org/press-releases/incorrect-projections-cause-campaign-costs-to-skyrocket/

16 "Gerrymander," *Oxford Dictionaries*, http://www.oxforddictionaries.com/us/definition/american_english/gerrymander.

exercise in voter disenfranchisement designed to protect incumbents and political parties.

**Modern Congress**

Today members of Congress have voted themselves an annual base salary of $174,000. Additionally they are given some very generous taxpayer-provided perks. For example, according to the 2014 Congressional Research Services (CRS) report on congressional salaries and allowances, the average annual compensation for a Senator's Official Personnel and Office Expense Account (SOPOEA) is an eye-popping $3,209,992. House Members scrape by on $1,243,560 per year. But there's more. Incumbents have given themselves wide latitude on what they can use campaign funds for. They can, for instance, use those funds to pay their rent, or they can put family members and girlfriends on the payroll. Peter Schweizer's book *Extortion: How Politicians Extract Your Money, Buy Votes and Line Their Own Pockets* details example after head-shaking example of what has been called "legal corruption." Go pick up Schweitzer's book; it's a firecracker of a read; just keep your blood pressure pills within arm's reach.

With virtual impunity, corruption is usually not far behind. The frequency of scandals in the nation's capitol is so common and ramifications so rare it is no wonder Main Street America is disgusted with the political system. Politicians quite simply live by their own set of rules. For example, there is Congressmen Charlie Rangel, Democrat from New York. Mr. Rangel has been in Congress for forty-four years. The very rules he made apparently don't apply to him. Rangel says that he forgot to pay several years of taxes on his luxury beachside villa that he owns in the Dominican Republic. He also forgot to report bank accounts in excess of $500,000, and he was further charged with an array of other tax and income-hiding charges.

**John Dingell—**
**Career Politician Deluxe**

In February 2013, members of Congress held a ceremony recognizing Congressman John Dingell as the longest-serving member of Congress. Dingell, a Democrat from Michigan, was first elected in 1955. Dwight Eisenhower was president, a gallon of gas cost about a quarter, and three pennies got you a postage stamp. No one had heard of the Beatles and nobody knew where Vietnam was. Mr. Dingell inherited his seat from his father, who was elected in 1923. The current Congressman Dingell intends to hand his seat off to his wife, Debbie Dingell, a former lobbyist for General Motors (that's how Dingell met her). His fellow congressmen are sad over his departure—what a loss to the House, to his district, and to Michigan, they say. And how has his state and district, which includes part of the city of Detroit, fared under his tenure? Well, Michigan is in dire financial straits, and Detroit is in shambles. What was once one of the most successful, beautiful cities in the world, Detroit has had to declare bankruptcy. The auto industry limps along in Detroit, while flourishing in business-friendly southern states.

At the time, Congressman Rangel was chairman of the powerful House Ways and Means Committee, the entity that is responsible for writing the very same tax code that he ignored. His punishment? He was "censured" by Congress, a toothless gesture that took all of about five minutes. Rangel is still hanging around, about to hit the half-century mark of time in congress. And if you're wondering how in the world he keeps getting reelected, ask yourself how a poor young man from Harlem somehow amassed the financial wherewithal to own beachside villas in the Caribbean alongside multiple six-figure bank accounts on a government salary.

Good-time Charlie certainly isn't alone in his misdeeds; he's just one pebble on the beach of career politicians who know how to game the system and get away with zero consequences for their actions. In fact the list of bad actors in Congress is as bipartisan as it is legion. Author Peter Schweizer, whom

City services are nonexistent, and the police department has issued warnings about the risks of even venturing into the city. Meanwhile, Mr. Dingell has amassed a net worth north of $7 million to show for his career as a politician. With his wife taking over his seat, the family fortune will no doubt continue to grow. How's that working for you, Detroit?

I mentioned above, also wrote *Throw Them All Out: How politicians and their friends get rich off insider trading tips, land deals, and cronyism that would send the rest of us to prison.* I challenge anyone to read this book and not come away in energetic support of congressional term limits.

**Government-Designed "Life Plans"**

Here's my inescapable disclaimer for this chapter: not all congressmen are dishonest and corrupt. Many are honorable men and women who go to DC with the best of intentions. However, no one is irreplaceable; it isn't as if the republic would collapse if, God forbid, after a decade or so they were to go back to where they came from and live under the laws that they passed. Surely those same Members of Congress would still be just as high minded with term limits, would they not? Moreover, what often happens is that after they get a few terms under their belts and get comfy in Washington they start to undergo a shift in their perspective. Instead of explaining their respective constituencies to the government, they wind up explaining government to their constituencies. At some point, every problem in America starts to look like a nail, and the federal government is the hammer. Low income and poverty is a problem in America? Right. Let's create a government program that will eradicate poverty, pass it into law, fund it, and hire more government workers to run it. At present there are over ninety separate means-tested government programs out there to address poverty, but guess what? Poverty rates in America today are virtually the same as they were when LBJ declared a War on Poverty over fifty years ago. Hmm, what to do, Congress wonders. How about *another* government program?

In July 2014, House Budget Committee Chairman and former vice presidential candidate Paul Ryan released his anti-poverty proposal entitled "Expanding Opportunity in America." In it he details his pilot proposal, called the "Opportunity Grant." It includes state and federal governments working together on the following:

In the envisioned scenario providers would work with families to design a customized life plan to provide a structured roadmap out of poverty. When crafting a life plan, they would include, at a minimum:

- A contract outlining specific and measurable benchmarks for success
- A timeline for meeting these benchmarks
- Sanctions for breaking the terms of the contract
- Incentives for exceeding the terms of the contract
- Time limits for remaining on cash assistance[17]

So here we have Paul Ryan, a Republican who ostensibly supports limited government, proposing that government bureaucrats sit down with families to create a "life plan." Really? A custom-made, government-supervised *life plan*? In America? Nothing personal against Mr. Ryan; he's a brilliant, well-meaning gentleman who pours his heart into his work and no doubt really wants to help poor people. To his credit, Expanding Opportunity in America does recommend consolidating the plethora of existing welfare programs as well as encouraging extensive federal-state coordination on those plans. But that's still a public sector, government-centric solution, and it is exactly my point: career politicians, even Republicans like

---

17 Paul Ryan, "Expanding Opportunity in America," July 24, 2014, http://budget.house.gov/uploadedfiles/expanding_opportunity_in_america.pdf. 17.

Ryan, sooner or later begin to look at everything through the prism of government. And Representative Ryan, like so many others in Congress, has spent his entire adult life in government, working as a Hill staffer for a number of years until he was elected to office at age twenty-eight. His official website paulryan.house.gov notes that at some point in his earlier life he worked in his family construction business back home in Wisconsin. Perhaps Mr. Ryan, along with any and all other career politicians in Washington, might benefit from returning to the private sector, producing goods and services, and signing paychecks. Then we might start to hear phrases such as "roll up your sleeves," and "take responsibility for your actions" out of Washington instead of, "You didn't build that." The ever succinct George Will put it thusly: "Term limits would increase the likelihood that people who come to Congress would anticipate returning to careers in the private sector and therefore would, as they legislate, think about what it is to live under the laws they make."

**Executive Tenure**

Here's some perspective on job tenure. The founders rejected the notion of an elite class of professional politicians running the government. That's why George Washington set an important precedent by walking away from the presidency after two terms. And they were right. This is a common approach in other career paths that come with great responsibility. For example, American military leaders spend an average of two to four years in their commands before moving on to another assignment. These officers are literally responsible for the lives of their subordinates and for millions or even billions of dollars worth of equipment, not to mention the security of the nation. Our armed forces long ago realized that parking an officer or noncommissioned officer in the same billet year after year, decade after decade, would be detrimental to the combat readiness, morale, and cohesion of the unit. Without a change

**Arlen Spector: Republican, Democrat, Whatever It Takes to Stay in Congress**

Arlen Spector was a staunch Republican politician in Pennsylvania for forty-four years. He was first elected to the US Senate in 1980. In 1995 he was even a Republican candidate for president, and was supported by fellow Pennsylvania Senator Rick Santorum, who is as Republican as they come. In 2010 with his reelection in jeopardy, rumors began to swirl that Spector was going to run as an Independent in order to avoid a tough primary challenge. However, Spector quashed that rumor, telling the *Philadelphia Inquirer* on March 18, 2009, that: "To eliminate any doubt, I am a Republican, and I am running for reelection in 2010 as a Republican on the Republican ticket." Oh yeah? Just over a month later, on April 28, Spector said this: "As the Republican Party has moved farther and farther to the right, I have found myself increasingly at odds with the Republican philosophy and more in line with the philosophy of the Democratic Party." What? Spector,

in leadership, both unit and leader become stale, and innovation and initiative grind to a halt.

The private sector also has frequent turnover in senior leadership. According to Yahoo Finance, the average tenure for a Fortune 500 CEO is about four and a half years.[18] These are the most prosperous, innovative companies in the world, and they make a point of turning over their leadership because they understand that fresh leadership brings fresh ideas and new perspective that propel their success.

But not in Congress, where once in, members can and do stay around pretty much as long as they like, to the detriment of just about everyone but themselves. Fresh ideas? Nope. An innovative approach? Please. Consider Alaska Senator Ted Stevens, the Republican Party's

[18] Gary Burnison, "The CEO Pay Circus of 2013," *Yahoo Finance*, March 21, 2013, http://finance.yahoo.com/blogs/the-exchange/ceo-pay-circus-2013-214028626.html.

a lifelong Republican and barely five weeks after publicly reaffirming his Republican *bona fides*, suddenly decides he is a liberal. Turns out that Spector was facing a tough primary challenge from Pat Toomey, so rather than lose, Spector decided he was a Democrat after all. All that mattered to Spector was getting reelected, even if it meant committing political treason and joining his political adversaries. One wonders what went through the hearts and minds of the millions of Pennsylvania voters who had supported him, contributed to, and volunteered for his campaigns throughout his decades as a Republican. Not surprisingly, the Pennsylvania Democrat Party welcomed Spector with open arms and overwhelmingly backed him as their nominee. Voters however, were having none of "Senator Turncoat" and soundly defeated him.

longest-serving senator, clocking in at forty-one years. Senator Stevens was the chairman of the Senate Committee on Commerce, Science, and Transportation, responsible, among other things, for regulating the Internet, which during a 2006 hearing, the eighty-three-year-old senator described as "a series of tubes."[19]

**The Republican Party and Big Government**

This section could just as easily be written into chapter 3, "The Problem with Big Government." However it is included here in the chapter on term limits because the argument has been made from the Right that neither an Article V Convention of States nor term limits would be necessary *if we would just elect the right people*. So just keep making that frontal assault we're told; elect more conservatives, the logic goes, and the problem takes care of itself. As a conservative, I really wish this were true. Unfortunately, the preponderance of evidence points to another conclusion, and that is that career politicians, regardless of party, will inevitably expand government. In fact it is painful to examine the establishment wing

19 "Ted Stevens," *Wikipedia*, http://en.wikipedia.org/wiki/Ted_Stevens#Committees_and_leadership_positions.

of the Republican Party's record when it comes to standing up for the conservative holy trinity of limited government, individual liberty, and free markets. Because for the most part, other than talking a good game on Fox news, they're AWOL. It turns out that the establishment wing of the Republican Party, which I define as the bulk of the Republicans who hold elective office in Washington those who run the party and the legions of consultants, fundraisers, *et al* who comprise the industry of politics, are complicit with, and benefit from, the expansion of government authority and all of the civic disease that comes with it. Paul Ryan's plan for government-designed "life plans" described earlier in this chapter is an example of that. There are many, many more, as we are about to see. When you learn to ignore the rhetoric, follow the money, and focus upon what they do, Republicans are up to their collective necks in growing government and of the crony capitalism that helps keep them in power. Call them Democrat lite, RINOs (Republicans In Name Only), whatever. The bottom line is that they're part of the powerful professional political class double-parked inside the Beltway that is robbing future generations of the American dream.

What's worse is that in so many ways establishment Republican complicity is arguably more caustic than the Democrats. Everyone knows what progressives are all about. As Reagan famously said: "It isn't that liberals are ignorant. It's just that they know so many things that aren't so," such as the liberal belief that we can tax ourselves rich or their blind obedience to a big government nanny state. But the thing is that they don't try to hide who they are. Just read a column (if you can stand it) by *New York Times* columnist Paul workers-of-the-world-unite Krugman, or just tune in to Obama, Pelosi, or Debbie Wasserman-Shultz; they'll tell you what they're about (election cycles notwithstanding). Democrat voters support liberal candidates because they promise that they're going to roll up their sleeves and make all of that juicy big government, social justice, kum-ba-yah utopia happen. When was the last time you heard a Democrat grouse about government having gotten too big, or that Americans really are paying *more* than our fair share of taxes? You'll never hear Senator Elizabeth Warren say to a small business owner; "Congratulations, *you* built that!" That's because liberal politicians and progressives are the intellectual descendants of Karl Marx and Vladimir Lenin, and they channel Saul Alinsky in word and deed. What's the difference between Socialists, Progressives, Democrats, and Marxists? Spelling.

Ahh, but Republicans are supposed to be different. They're supposed to be the intellectual descendants of our Founding Fathers, and they channel Milton Friedman in word and deed. Those are the principles championed by their conservative base across America. Those are also the views of the majority of Republican governors throughout the nation, and those are certainly the views of the Tea Party movement. So why does the establishment wing of the Republican Party go brain dead on these principles once they put down roots inside of the Beltway? Like any politician, they talk a good game, but when the Fox News TV camera lights blink off and the makeup gets scrubbed away, what are we really left with?

**How Establishment Republicans Govern**

From 2001 to 2006 there was a Republican Yatzee in Washington. Republicans owned the White House, the Senate, and the House. What came from that? Did they reform entitlements, shrink government, and reduce the national debt? Hardly. Instead Republicans created a brand new entitlement, Medicare Part D. They grew government, creating a huge new federal entity called the Department of Homeland Security, which is now the third largest federal government agency. They established a vast federal education mandate called No Child Left Behind. The national debt ballooned by 86 percent ($5.7 trillion to $10.6 trillion from 2000 to 2008). Balanced budgets were nowhere to be found, and Republicans blew through debt ceilings faster than Chuck Yeager ripping through the sound barrier. Federal regulations? Republicans spewed out federal regulations like a hung-over frat boy after a weekend in Tijuana. The Federal Registry, the official record that lists all government regulations, topped out at over seventy-nine thousand pages under our last Republican president, barely a smidgeon under President Obama's high-water mark of about eighty-two thousand pages.

There are plenty of other examples, such as Richard Nixon's wage and price controls or his creation of the regulatory Brown Shirts that comprise the Environmental Protection Agency (EPA). The clear exception to viable Republican governance in Washington was Reagan, but then no one ever mistook him for being an Establishment Republican. And that's the point. It is also the mistaken quest that most conservatives have come to seek in elective politics. Because sadly, most of what Reagan accomplished, including tax cuts, unprecedented job growth and scaled back regulations has been gradually undone by a combination of Republicans and Democrats alike, starting with his successor George Herbert Walker Bush. "Read my lips, no new taxes." Ouch. It seems as if Republicans (Reagan excepted) hate big government unless they're in charge of it.

In order to stay popular and stay in office, Republicans have largely conceded the battlefield of ideas to Democrats. Why aren't Republicans out there articulating and debating conservative values? Liberals define the terms and control the debate in Washington. Whether it is blanket amnesty for illegal aliens, new entitlements and more entitlement spending, contraception, minimum wage, how much to hike taxes, slashing the defense budget, reductions to veterans' benefits, global cooling/warming/climate change, whatever the issue, progressives live rent free inside of establishment Republicans' heads.

## United Against the Tea Party

> **Liberal Quotes Concerning the Tea Party**
>
> "They (the Tea Party) have acted like terrorists."
> —Vice President of the United States Joe Biden (D, RI)
>
> "The Tea Party can go straight to Hell."
> —Congresswoman Maxine Waters (D, CA)
>
> "It is the same group we faced in the South with those white crackers and the dogs and the police."
> —Congressman Charlie Rangel (D, NY)
>
> "Unhinged Arsonists"
> —DNC Chair Debbie Wasserman-Schultz (D, FL)
>
> "Insane People Who Have Lost their Minds"
> —Senate Majority Leader Harry Reid (D, NV)
>
> "People with a Bomb Strapped to their Chest"
> —Deputy White House Spokesman Dan Pfeiffer
>
> "Blatant Extortionists"
> —White House Spokesman Jay Carney
>
> "Legislative Arsonists"
> —House Minority Leader Nancy Pelosi (D, CA)

The Tea Party movement was viciously and gleefully attacked from the Left, starting with President Obama and coursing all the way down through rank and file Democrats. Naturally the progressive push-up bra that is the mainstream media also went apoplectic over the Tea Party.

No real surprises so far. After all, the Tea Party articulated simple, time-honored conservative principles such as adhering to the Constitution, reducing taxes, shrinking government, and maintaining a strong military. In other words, "radical extremists" according to the Left. With all of the liberal over-the-top rhetoric, one would naturally expect that establishment Republicans would take the opposite tact and embrace their base, right? Well, not so much. The establishment wing of the Republican Party had very little love for the Tea Party either. The public comments weren't nearly as vicious or hateful as what came from the Left, but after 2010 it became very clear that establishment Republicans, including leaders like Senate Minority Leader Mitch McConnell, Senator John McCain, Speaker of the House John Boehner, House Majority Leader Eric Cantor, and Representative Peter King had very little use for the Tea Party. Congressman King actually started an anti-Tea Party PAC to support non-Tea Party Republicans. This internecine fight reached its nadir in the 2014 senate primary in Mississippi, where establishment Republicans rallied behind one of their own, spending millions of dollars supporting Thad Cochran—not against a Democrat opponent, but against another Republican—State Senator and Tea Party-backed Chris McDaniel! The Republican Party's onslaught of attack ads, mailings, and robo-calls were actually aimed to get out the African American Democrat vote against McDaniel, implying he was a racist who hated Barack Obama. And sure enough, the Democrat vote was just enough to put Cochran over the top. Shortly after the race, the Congressional Black Caucus came calling, making it known that they expected some payback from Cochran on a litany of traditionally liberal issues. Cochran, who is seventy-six and has been in congress since Nixon was president no doubt knows how to play that all-too-typical insider game of mutual back scratch with taxpayer dollars. Some victory, Republicans.

This isn't necessarily meant to lionize the Tea Party. Like any group, they have had good candidates and ideas, others not so good; in other words, they are human. But the inescapable

**Establishment GOP Views of the Tea Party**

"I think we are going to crush them (Tea Party) everywhere. I don't think they are going to have a single nominee anywhere in the country."
—Senate Minority Leader Mitch McConnell (R, KY)

"The problem with the Tea Party, I think it's just unsustainable because they can never come up with a coherent vision for governing the country. It will die out."
—Senator Lindsey Graham (R, SC)

> "Wacko birds;" referring to Tea Party favorites Senator Marco Rubio, Senator Rand Paul, Representative Justin Amash.
>
> —Senator John McCain (R, AZ)
>
> "If you look underneath the surface of the Tea Party movement you will find that it is not sophisticated. It's not like these people have read the economist Friedrich August von Hayek."
>
> —Karl Rove
>
> "I'm looking at this (running for president) because I see people like Rand Paul and Ted Cruz, and to me, I don't want the Republican Party going in that direction."
>
> —Representative Peter King (R, NY)

fact is that they are the natural base of the Republican Party, frustrated that no matter who they send to Washington all they get back are higher taxes and bigger government. Instead of embracing them, the establishment wing of the party gave them the back of their hand.

That brings us to the "teachable moment" of this section, which is what transpired when an outside entity threatened the status quo inside of the Beltway. When that happened, The professional political class in Washington, Democrats and Republicans alike united to preserve their incumbencies. For the most part it worked. With the exception of Cantor, who lost to a motivated Tea Party candidate and constituency in the primary, all the establishment guys are still there. This is a bitter pill if you are part of the Republican base living and working across this great land. It leaves you feeling like there is no one who represents your views. Establishment Republicans seem to be willing to accept bigger government, higher taxes, more regulations, national mandates on education, blanket amnesty, and even cutting veterans' benefits as long as it keeps them in office. This is reflected in public opinion: According to Rasmussen polling, 53 percent of self-described Democrat voters approve of their elected representatives, while only 28 percent of likely Republican voters believe that Republicans in

Congress are doing a good job standing up for conservative values.[20] This explains the growing rift in the Republican Party and why GOP voter turnout has become increasingly problematic in national elections. Interestingly, during this same timeframe, the number of Republican governors and Republican state representatives throughout the country has increased. So it isn't that conservative beliefs are on the wane, quite the contrary. The fault line runs through the political system and on the political Right it is a chasm separating conservatives and establishment Republicans that will continue to grow.

## Twenty-First Century America, Brought to You by Career Politicians

Career politicians are now a central component of the political culture in Washington to the detriment to the country. The American norm used to be one of unbridled optimism, an expectation of robust economic growth, job opportunity, higher wages, strong national defense, and social safety nets as opposed to government-provided hammocks. Success. Dream big and go make it happen. But now, in the twenty-first century, we're told by establishment politicians that the new "norm" of America is mediocrity. GDP growth is tepid at best, the economy isn't expanding, yet the government continues to grow. Over 100 million Americans are out of the workforce. Taxes stay high yet we're informed that we need to pay even more because those same politicians can't stop spending. There is zero political courage from the Right or desire from the Left to pursue tax reform, much less entitlement reform. Our armed forces are being hollowed out. Veterans are kicked to the curb. Millennials may not have figured it out yet, but they are going to be the ones to deal with massive federal debt

---

20 "GOP Voters Think Republicans in Congress out of Touch," *Rasmussen Reports*, September 24, 2014, http://www.rasmussenreports.com/public_content/politics/general_politics/september_2014/gop_voters_think_republicans_in_congress_out_of_touch.

piled on top of trillions in student loan debt and about $100 trillion in unfunded entitlement mandates. Good luck with that. Inflation and high interest rates are coming. Oh, by the way, there aren't any jobs, and what's the solution from the government? Legalize millions of illegal aliens. The American dream and the drive to provide a better, more secure future for the next generation, is in danger.

## Government-Sponsored Civil Unrest

Thanks to our expansive government and career politicians, America is on the verge of becoming an also-ran nation, which qualifies as a tragedy given the unlimited potential brought about by limited government, individual liberty, and a free market economy. Neil Young sang, "it is better to burn out than to fade away." Well not when it comes to government, particularly when it is self-inflicted. Fading away, turning into the Mediocre States of America is bad enough, but the potential of a burnout is much, much worse. Americans have been told that their government is going to take care of them. Indeed welfare and food stamp recipients are at all-time highs under Obama. In 2014, over 110 million Americans rely predominately upon government welfare for their subsistence. Presently the government is sitting on top of about $100 trillion in unfunded mandates (that is, promises made by career politicians that the government can't keep). So what is going to happen when the almost fifty million people who have EBT cards (high-tech food stamps) are told that their cards are only going to be refilled at pennies on the dollar? Or when the 110 million people on welfare are told that the money is gone. How about the millions more who are recipients of Social Security, Medicare, veterans' benefits and pensions, and government employee benefits and pensions. What is going to happen when the government shrugs its shoulders and announces that pennies on the dollar is the best they can do? We've already discussed Detroit as a harbinger of things to come. The recent riots in Greece over government pension cuts are another example, although it will be much, much worse here in America. Sure the government can just print more money, but we know what comes with that—hyperinflation. Most affluent Americans have seen the writing on the wall, and already have escape plans in place for themselves, their families, and their wealth. Also, as we will see in the next chapter, the government is now weaponized on the domestic front. It is an ugly scenario that is shaping up. The rest of us had best get ready, because it's coming, folks, sooner than later, unless we do something now.

**US Congress: Millionaires Club**

Main Street America might be struggling—jobs are hard to find and the nation is over $17 trillion in debt—but the financial situation has never been better for members of Congress. According to 2012 financial disclosure forms, for the first time in American history, the majority of members of Congress have a net worth exceeding $1 million. *Median* net worth for all members of Congress is $1,008,767. I guess that's what they mean by "government by the wealthy."[21]

Restoring American exceptionalism entails repairing, to the greatest extent possible, America's core principles as articulated in the Constitution. But it is clear that a roadmap back to those core principles will never come from the Left. And if the establishment wing of the Republican Party is complicit in government expansion, growing debt, higher taxes, and crony capitalism, then it becomes axiomatic that restoring America will never come from inside of the Beltway. That means we must pop the Beltway bubble from the outside, by imposing congressional term limits and, as we will see in the following chapter, a balanced-budget amendment. The mechanism for this is a Convention of States as depicted in Article V of the Constitution.

[21] Russ Choma, "Millionaires' Club: For First Time, Most Lawmakers are Worth $1 Million-Plus," *Open Secrets*, January 9, 2014, http://www.opensecrets.org/news/2014/01/millionaires-club-for-first-time-most-lawmakers-are-worth-1-million-plus/.

# CHAPTER 3

# The Federal Government: A Weaponized Parasite

## The Growth of Government

It was a lovely spring day in Philadelphia, May 15, 1800, when President John Adams issued the order for the federal government of the United States of America to pack up and relocate from its Philadelphia digs to the nation's more-or-less completed national capital of Washington city. At that point the federal government consisted of the Departments of State, Treasury, and War, employing all of about 125 people. Today a single Walmart Supercenter would dwarf that.[22] So it didn't take long to pack the federal government into a series of wagons in order to make the trek from Philadelphia to Washington on the banks of the Potomac River. Exactly one month later, on June 15, so the story goes, the government was back up and operating in the new capital. In a letter to her sister, First Lady Abigail Adams described a portion of her carriage trip:

> I arrived in this city on Sunday the 16th. Having lost my way in the woods on Saturday in going from Baltimore, we took the road to Frederick and got nine miles out of our road. You

22 "Our Story," Walmart Corporation, http://corporate.walmart.com/our-story/locations/united-states

> find nothing but a forest & woods on the way, for 16 and 18 miles not a village. Here and there a thatched cottage without a single pane of glass.[23]

Today that same region of Maryland, along with neighboring Northern Virginia, is sprawling suburbs of gleaming glass, steel, and clogged highways that snuggle up to Washington, an opportunistic buffer surrounding the richest, most powerful city in the history of the world. This Beltway Bubble operates according to its own exclusive economic and political ecosystem, a federal manifest destiny largely impervious to the normal fiscal and economic laws applicable everywhere else in the country. For example, the 2008 economic crisis that devastated so much of the country, unceremoniously tossed millions of homeowners upside down in their mortgages, triggered millions of foreclosures and massive job losses in the private sector, gutted savings, devastated 401(k)s and other investments, barely created a ripple in the National Capitol region. The government-centric economy hummed along; few if any jobs were lost and property values held firm. In other words, Party on, Garth. This plays out quite clearly in the differences of opinion between Washington insiders and the rest of the American public when asked about the direction of the country. A 2010 Politico poll revealed that while only 27 percent of the American public at large believed the country was going in the right direction, 49 percent of DC insiders thought that the country was on the right track.[24] If that's not enough, try and wrap your brain around this: *five out of the top six wealthiest counties in America are Washington suburbs*. How is that possible considering the fact that the federal government produces exactly nothing of value? Say thank-you to the American taxpayer, who provides this

---

23 "President John Adams orders federal government to Washington, DC," *History*, http://www.history.com/this-day-in-history/president-john-adams-orders-federal-government-to-washington-dc.

24 Andy Barr, "Poll: D.C. elites a world apart," *Politico*, July 18, 2010, http://www.politico.com/news/stories/0710/39809.html.

unprecedented largesse. The federal government is a taker, not a maker. Big time.

**Wealthiest Counties in America**[25]

| Rank | County | State | Median Income |
|---|---|---|---|
| 1 | Loudoun County* | Virginia | $117,876 |
| 2 | Howard County* | Maryland | $108,844 |
| 3 | Fairfax County* | Virginia | $107,096 |
| 4 | Hunterdon County | New Jersey | $105,186 |
| 5 | Arlington County* | Virginia | $100,474 |
| 6 | Stafford County* | Virginia | $97,606 |

* Washington, DC, suburbs

What's wrong with this picture? America's founders were intimately familiar with the inevitable oppressive nature of large, powerful government and of those who wield that power. That's why they sought to constrain government and (therefore) to maximize individual liberty. The Constitution provided a tightly scripted role for government while empowering the individual with ample leeway for *ad lib*. But now those roles have reversed, dangerously so. The federal government of the twenty-first century has become the very thing the founders feared, actually much worse. That humble little band of 125 government workers who set up shop in 1800 has mutated into a weaponized parasite of untold size that is consuming the wealth, productivity, and liberty of the citizenry it was created to serve.

At some level, Americans comprehend the ramifications of this role reversal; call it a "liberty gene" that comes with our national birthright. However busy lives, reality TV, and an all-too-understandable gag reflex to anything political precludes connecting the dots. So let's do that here. Observe two key public opinion polls. First, in the "Right Direction or Wrong Track" polls, we see that anywhere from 70

[25] "List of Highest Income Counties in the United States," 2012 American Community Survey, *Wikipedia*, **http://en.wikipedia.org/wiki/List_of_highest-income_counties_in_the_United_States**.

percent to 80 percent of the American public consistently believe the country is on the wrong track.[26] Next, look at Gallup's "Most Important Problem" poll,[27] which asks Americans to list their biggest concerns. The overwhelming majority of those concerns have the government's fingerprints all over them, including:

| | |
|---|---|
| Economy in general: | 20% |
| Dissatisfaction with government: | 19% |
| Immigration/illegal aliens: | 13% |
| Unemployment/jobs: | 12% |
| Federal budget/debt: | 5% |
| Education: | 4% |
| National security | 3% |
| Welfare: | 2% |
| Lack of military defense: | 1% |
| Judicial system: | 1% |
| Taxes: | 1% |
| Elections/election reform | 1% |

When we add up the percentages of those things that concern Americans most that are government related, the total comes to 82 percent, which mirrors the percentage of Americans who believe the country is on the wrong track. Overlapping those two polls, without explicitly saying so, Americans understand that government is the problem. It might be dormant, but that's a liberty gene.

---

26 "Right Direction or Wrong Track," *Rasmussen Reports*, http://www.rasmussenreports.com/public_content/politics/mood_of_america/right_direction_or_wrong_track.

27 "Most Important Problem," *Gallup*, November 6-9, 2014, http://www.gallup.com/poll/1675/most-important-problem.aspx.

Say you're the parent of a petulant teenaged girl with a strong sense of entitlement who is absolutely certain she knows pretty much everything. She won't listen, and she won't work. She feels completely justified in spending your money, blowing through every dime of the allowance you give her, lying to you, and then demanding more. If you balk, she guilt trips you that you're greedy, that you aren't paying your "fair share." She insists that the debt limit on her credit cards be raised, over and over again. She borrows money from friends and neighbors, whoever has a dime. She is literally bankrupting your family, but she just doesn't seem to care. Our destructive teen's name is "Congress." The only way to modify the behavior of Congress is to administer some tough love, starting with taking away the credit card and slashing the allowance. Congress, the one in our national capitol, holds the nation's purse strings. By forcing career politicians to only spend tax dollars within a tightly scripted, balanced budget, it becomes possible to arrest government expansion and begin to pay down the crushing debt. It won't happen overnight, but then this debacle wasn't created overnight either. Also, we must realize that reining in government will never come voluntarily from within government itself. Career politicians in both parties have too much to lose by self-limiting. But how did this happen? How did the federal government devolve from that limited role explicitly created and articulated in the Constitution into the weaponized regulatory monstrosity that it has become? Read on.

## FDR and the New Deal: Government on Steroids

As detailed in chapter 2 when we discussed career politicians, the growth of government began in earnest with the election of hard-core progressive Woodrow Wilson and the legalization of a federal income tax. Once that threshold was breached, President Franklin Delano Roosevelt set out to make every American dependent upon, and/or answerable to, the federal government. Prechanneling

Obama's former Chief of Staff Rahm Emmanuel's adage to "never let a crisis go to waste," FDR ran on a "New Deal," whereby massive government intervention would supposedly lift America out of the Great Depression. FDR created dozens of new governmental regulatory agencies, many of which the Supreme Court ultimately declared unconstitutional.

**Porn for Progressives: FDR's Alphabet Soup of Federal Agencies**

NRA – National Recovery Act

ERA – Emergency Relief and Construction Act

AAA – Agricultural Adjustment Act

FERA – Federal Emergency Relief Administration

WPA – Works Progress Administration (a.k.a. "We Piddle Around")

CCC – Civilian Conservation Corps

CWA – Civilian Works Administration

PWA – Public Works Administration

TVA – Tennessee Valley Authority

He implemented wage and price controls, dictated which sectors of the economy could produce and how much, and which sectors couldn't. Kind of like a Soviet Five Year Plan. In order for the government to pay for everything, FDR went all in on tax collections. As discussed in the previous chapter, the ratification of the Sixteenth Amendment in 1913 enabled the first federal income taxes. Those initial rates were a modest 1 percent on the first $20,000 of taxable income and 7 percent on incomes above $500,000. In today's dollars, that would amount to 1 percent on the first $466,098 of taxable income and 7 percent on incomes over $11,652,450. That sounds pretty good, but as we know now, those rates changed. Less than thirty years later, in 1942 FDR signed an executive order taxing all income over $25,000 at a rate of 100 percent. That comes to about $376k in today's money. You and make over that and Washington gets *all of it*. Some incentive, huh? Well, congress balked and worked out a "compromise" rate of 90 percent over $25k, along with a 20 percent rate for anything over $500, or about $7,517 today.[28] Sheesh.

How did the New Deal work out? It is certainly conventional wisdom about FDR in academia and on the Left that all of that big government brought America out of the Great Depression. Scratch a Democrat or a political science professor in just about any university in America and they'll be happy to tell you how FDR brought us out of the Depression.

However, it isn't as clean and dry as depicted. Even President Roosevelt's own inner circle had serious misgivings, including FDR's own Treasury secretary. In a confessional moment likely born out of frustration, Henry Morgenthau Jr., FDR's Treasury secretary, who was also his closest friend, said the following while testifying before the House Ways and Means Committee in May 1939, after seven years in office:

> We have tried spending money. We are spending more than we have ever spent before and it does not work. And I have just one interest, and if I am wrong … somebody else can have my job. I want to see this country prosperous. I want to see people get a job. I want to see people get enough to eat. We have never made good on our promises … I say after eight years of this Administration we have just as much unemployment as when we started … And an enormous debt to boot!"[29]

---

28 "Inflation Calculator," *Dollar Times*, http://www.dollartimes.com/inflation/inflation.php?amount.

29 Burton Folsom, Jr., *New Deal or Raw Deal? How FDR's Economic Legacy has Damaged America* (New York: Threshold, 2008), 2.

FDR had a lot on his plate from the Great Depression to World War II. Not to mention his personal cross of polio where just getting out of bed in the morning was a crucible. Despite all of that he had a way of giving Americans hope for the future. Hell, Reagan even voted for him all four times.[30] But hindsight is twenty-twenty, and government was not the answer to all our problems then, or now. Perhaps FDR's famous quote that "The only thing we have to fear is ... fear itself." should have been "The only thing we have to fear is ... our government."

**LBJ's Great Society and the War on Poverty: More Government becomes more Massive, Failed Social Welfare**

Here we are in America, fifty years into that big War on Poverty declared by President Johnson in 1964. So I'm a soldier and war has been declared. What does that really mean? What is the mission, who is the enemy, what are we going to do about t? Explore LBJ's programs. Twenty-one trillion US tax dollars have been spent across over ninety separate government programs handing out cash, food, housing, health care, drugs, phones, and various other social services. However, the poverty rate in 2014 is virtually the same as it was when the program started in 1964, and now we are spending over $1 trillion annually. The Left's War on Poverty has been a colossal failure by virtually every statistical metric imaginable. So those are the numbers. Just some digits, right? But behind those numbers is the all too real devastating human impact it has had, to include the destruction of the African American family unit. Today the single most important factor impacting the success or failure of a child is whether he or she is born outside of marriage. The percentages before and after LBJ's War on Poverty are startling. As Jennifer Marshall of the Heritage Foundation points out in "How to Fight Poverty—and Win: "When the War on Poverty began, 8 percent of all children in America were born outside marriage. Since the

30 Reagan, *An American Life*, 316.

mid-'60s, unwed childbearing has skyrocketed to more than 40 percent of all births, and from 25 percent to about 73 percent among black children." As well meaning as big government provided social justice proponents may be, their solutions do not work, quite the opposite in fact. Our founders knew that, including George Washington when he said: "*A government is like fire, a handy servant, but a dangerous master.*"

## Community Organizer in Chief Barack Obama Using Government to Address "Deep Flaws" in the Constitution and American Culture

Much like his predecessor Woodrow Wilson, Obama has been highly critical of the Constitution. In a 2001 interview on a Chicago public radio program, Obama described the US Constitution as having "deep flaws" and said the country's Founding Fathers had "an enormous blind spot" when they wrote it. "I think it is an imperfect document, and I think it is a document that reflects some deep flaws in American culture"[31]

Throughout his 2008 presidential campaign, Obama repeatedly stressed his intention to "fundamentally transform America." Now the only reason to set out to fundamentally transform anything is if you believe it to be fundamentally flawed. In this way, both Wilson and Obama are presidential bookends in progressive politics. Both viewed the Constitution as flawed, and both believed that robust government action could redress those flaws. Both were fundamentally wrong.

---

31 David Patten, "Obama: Constitution is 'Deeply Flawed,'" *Newsmax*, October 27, 2008, http://www.newsmax.com/InsideCover/obama-constitution/2008/10/27/id/326165/.

## Government Gone Wild: A Regulatory State

Today, the progressive wet dream of a regulatory social welfare state is rapidly coming to fruition. What is manifestly clear is that it is a zero-sum game that is eclipsing the American dream. Individual liberty is, of necessity, vanishing. Americans subsist under a crushing layer of government laws, rules, regulations, edicts, and directives. Here is Michael Snyder's take on *Business Insider*:

> Today, the U.S. government has an "alphabet agency" for just about everything. The nanny state feels like it has to watch, track and tightly control virtually everything that we do. The Federal Register is the main source of regulations for U.S. government agencies. In 1936, the number of pages in the Federal Register was about 2,600. Today, the Federal Register is over 80,000 pages long. That is just one example of how bad things have gotten.[32]

Everything, be it animal, vegetable, or mineral, with which you interact from wake up until lights out, from birth to death, is subject to countless regulations. Alarm clocks, water taps, water, toilets, shower nozzles, appliances, electricity, heat, cooling, light bulbs, toothbrushes, toothpaste, food, drink, packaging, communications, cars, fuel, garage door openers, streets, signage, curbs, sidewalks, traffic lights, banks, mortgages, wages, schools, textbooks, curriculum, tests, teachers, health care, funeral homes, cemeteries, and everything else, the government regulates it and taxes it. Moreover, we now know that the government listens and/or records every phone call, text, tweet, e-mail, every pic or enclosure sent.

---

[32] Michael Snyder, "12 Ridiculous Government Regulations that are Almost too Bizarre to Believe," *Business Insider*, November 12, 2010, http://www.businessinsider.com/ridiculous-regulations-big-government-2010-11?op=1#ixzz32N330p96.

Just go check out the government's own website; www.regulations.gov if you dare. A quick search over a ninety-day period revealed that the government had produced over *six thousand* job-killing, liberty-erasing, income-expunging regulations, rules, proposed rules, notices, etc. All the usual suspects were there; the EPA, Energy, Education, Labor, Agriculture, Banking, Housing, telecommunications, the list goes on. And on. And on…

**The Cost of Regulations**

In his annual report "Ten Thousand Commandments" Clyde Wayne Crews documents some mind-blowing statistics:

- Since 1993 the government has had an annual outflow of over thirty-five hundred "final rules" for a total of 87,282 new rules.
- Regulatory compliance costs $1.863 *trillion* annually, equal to over 11 percent of GDP (US GDP in 2013 was $16.797 trillion).
- Regulatory compliance of $1.863 trillion exceeded income tax revenue of $1.234 trillion.
- Regulatory compliance of $1.863 trillion combined with federal spending of $3.454 trillion means the government accounts for 31 percent of the US economy.
- If US regulations were a country, it would be the tenth largest in the world, exceeding the GDPs of Australia and Canada.
- The annual cost of regulations to American households is $14,974. For an average household this amounts to more than any other expenditure except housing.
- The top rule-imposing agencies are the Departments of Treasury, Interior, Commerce, Transportation, and Health

and Human Services.[33] EPA, normally in the top five, is now sixth, edged out by HHS, no doubt thanks to Obamacare.

Eighty thousand-plus pages of rules and regulations, forever modified, added, tweaked, interpreted, and reinterpreted by an army of bureaucrats hardly bodes well for that old adage about ignorance of the law being no excuse, not to mention what it does to suffocate productivity. Eighty thousand-plus was the high-water mark under President Obama in 2010. By the end of 2013 the number had dropped to a "mere" 79,311 pages. While government regulations amount to catnip for liberals, it was really no better under Republican administrations. For example, in 2008, the last year of George W. Bush's presidency, the Federal Registry topped out at 79,435 pages, just a smidgeon under Obama's. And lest we forget, it was Republican President Richard Nixon who gave birth to the regulatory-happy EPA on December 2, 1970. Growing government is a bipartisan sport.

Before all of the straw man arguments crank up, the answer is yes, some regulations are useful, necessary, and worthwhile. No, I don't want dirty water and chewy air. But the volume of regulations coming at us now is just like the red wine analogy: research shows that a glass or two a day is actually good for you, but more isn't better. Regulation-wise, we're up to fifty, a hundred, bottles a day, if you get my meaning. In America, regulations have joined death and taxes on the short list of inevitability. And God help you if you get sideways with one of these agencies; when it comes to pushing regulations and pulling revenue, Uncle Sam don't play around.

---

33 Clyde Wayne Crews, "Ten Thousand Commandments 2014, an Annual Snapshot of the Federal Regulatory State," *Competitive Enterprise Institute*, April 29, 2014, https://cei.org/studies/ten-thousand-commandments-2014

## Weaponized Government: Soviet Power Ministries

During the Cold War, Western Sovietologists coined the phrase "Power Ministries" when alluding to the USSR's Ministries of Defense, Internal Affairs, and the KGB. The road to gaining and holding power inside Soviet Russia ran right through those Power Ministries. Soviet leaders needed these institutions behind them in order to maintain control through force or the threat of it, reward political allies and punish enemies, enforce regulations, and keep the money flowing in. Naturally it was critical for the government to keep very close tabs on the population. They bugged homes and offices, followed and filmed people, employed individuals to inform on their friends, family, and neighbors, and maintained a web of KGB officers throughout the country. The result was that everyone was vulnerable; everyone was subject to the whims of government power. If the Communist Party decided to come after you, they could create pretenses for doing so. Joseph Stalin kept his Power Ministries busy forcibly relocating, imprisoning, and murdering millions of his own citizens. Every Russian leader since then, up to and including President and ex-KGB agent Vladimir Putin, has continued to rely upon variations of the Power Ministries. Such is Russian political culture, and an inevitable offshoot of a powerful, expansive central government. In Russia there is not now, nor has there ever been, a right to privacy. Russia has no Bill of Rights, and no Fourth Amendment that protects the citizenry against "unreasonable searches and seizures." The concepts of limited government and individual liberty are as alien to Russian culture as NASCAR is to the Upper West Side of Manhattan.

## Weaponized Government: Power Ministries American Style

Americans, by contrast, do have an expectation of privacy. It is part of our national DNA and is right there in the Bill of Rights. However, the government has developed very different expectations. In fact, the "right of the people to be secure in their persons, houses, papers, and effects, against unreasonable searches and seizures" now means no more than what the federal government and those who control it decide that it means. Twenty-first century US government bristles with upgraded, high-tech, weaponized power ministries that can dig into our personal lives to a level about which Soviet leaders could only dream. Just like in the old Soviet Union, the US government's Power Ministries employ millions of people, operate on massive budgets, and retain substantial power and broad authority. Believe it or not, they also maintain substantial arsenals and security forces. The founders created a system of limited government that would empower individuals, not the government. But all of that has changed as a professional political class is increasingly willing to use power ministries, often bypassing the Constitution to do so. When political leaders can operate with virtual impunity, and stop playing by the rules, we get on a very slippery slope to a much more oppressive government. Indeed this is happening right now. The oath that career politicians take to support and defend the Constitution isn't worth the paper it is printed on. Instead it is much easier, much more convenient, and effective to use the power of the federal government to coerce, intimidate, and enforce.

**The Fourth Amendment to the Constitution**

The right of the people to be secure in their persons, houses, papers, and effects, against unreasonable searches and seizures, shall not be violated, and no warrants shall issue but upon probable cause, supported by oath or affirmation, and particularly describing the place to be searched, and the persons or things to be seized.

Whatever one may think of the actions of Edward Snowden, his leaks revealed the length to which the National Security Agency (NSA) spies on *all* American citizens. The NSA doesn't just collect data, it collects *metadata*. Glenn Greenwald, writing in the *National Post*, notes that "the NSA's own slogan which appears repeatedly throughout its own documents (is): '*collect it all.*'"[34] Paging George Orwell. By its own admission, the US government is collecting and storing massive amounts of metadata on every single American. Metadata isn't so much about listening in on your calls (they can do that too) as it is about putting together and storing a series of data points that actually can create a much more detailed picture of what an individual is doing beyond just a single conversation. As Daniel Amico explains in his article "Why NSA's Metadata Collection Should Disturb You," data points include call duration, call location, date and time of the call, who you called, and how long you spoke, as well as other identifiers.[35] Combined with your e-mails, tweets, and Internet search histories, records of your comings and goings, credit card purchases, etc., the NSA, and other agencies including the FBI, the IRS, and the EPA to name a few, can aggregate those data points and piece together exactly what is going on in your life, your political leanings, the organizations you belong to and support, to whom you give money, how much you're worth, where you go, what you do and with whom you are doing it. They can even tell what you are reading. In his terrific book *America: Imagine a World without Her*" Dinesh D'Sousa points out, "if you read this book electronically some government analyst at the NSA might be watching you do it." Whatever you're doing, no matter how you try to hide it, a good analyst can sift through your metadata and know what you are doing. The *Guardian* offered a simple case study of how metadata works using the scandal surrounding David Petraeus's affair with Paula Broadwell:

1. To communicate, Paula Broadwell and David Petraeus shared an anonymous e-mail account.

---

34 Glenn Greenwald, "The NSA's 'collect it all' mission," *National Post*, May 2, 2014, http://fullcomment.nationalpost.com/2014/05/02/glenn-greenwald-the-nsas-collect-it-all-mission/.

35 Daniel Amico, "Why NSA's 'Metadata' Collection Should Disturb You," *Freedomworks*, June 20, 2013, http://www.freedomworks.org/content/why-nsa's-"metadata"-collection-should-disturb-you.

2. Instead of sending e-mails, both would log in to the account, edit, and save drafts.
3. Broadwell logged in from various hotels' public Wi-Fi, leaving a trail of metadata that included times and locations.
4. The FBI cross-referenced hotel guests with log in times and locations, leading to the identification of Broadwell.[36]

All of this came out of the Patriot Act, which originated in the George W. Bush administration (and repeatedly approved by Congress since then) a response to the terrorist attacks of 9/11. Of course we all want to be safe, and indeed if anything is a core responsibility of the federal government, it is to "provide for the common defense." But the best way to do that is by strengthening our military capability, not by slathering on additional layers of government bureaucracy. Despite railing against the Patriot Act in the 2008 presidential campaign, the Obama administration has pocketed all of this overreach and has taken it to new levels. Remember: politicians and governments do not willingly give up power. Left unchecked, the next administration, Republican or Democrat, will do the exact same thing. The

| **Government Power Ministries** |
|---|
| Internal Revenue Service |
| National Security Agency |
| Environmental Protection Agency |
| Federal Bureau of Investigation |
| National Labor Relations Board |
| Bureau of Land Management |
| Department of Treasury |
| Department of Justice |
| Department of Labor |
| Department of Interior |
| Department of Commerce |
| Department of Transportation |
| Department of Health and Human Services |

36 "A Guardian Guide to Your Metadata," The Guardian, June 12, 2013, http://www.theguardian.com/technology/interactive/2013/jun/12/what-is-metadata-nsa-surveillance#meta=0000000.

metadata of every American is permanently stored in some giant government cloud, giving it the ability to intimidate, coerce, or prosecute anyone, anytime. But that could never happen, not in America, Right?

## Targeting Political Opponents

There's never a shortage of finger pointing, accusations, and posturing coming from our politicians, particularly during a campaign cycle. What has become alarming is the increasing willingness of career politicians in power to openly call for and employ government agencies against political opposition. In a speech to the Carter Center for American Progress in January 2014, New York Democrat Senator Chuck Schumer openly called for the Internal Revenue Service to be used to curtail Tea Party group funding in order to "exploit" and "weaken" the movement. Schumer believed that Tea Party groups somehow have a financial advantage owing to the Supreme Court's 2010 Citizens United decision, and therefore the Obama administration should ignore the Constitution, bypass Congress, and dictate new campaign finance rules through the IRS. "It is clear that we will not pass anything legislatively as long as the House of Representatives is in Republican control, *but there are many things that can be done administratively by the IRS and other government agencies*—we must redouble those efforts immediately," Schumer said.[37] Schumer was joined by Democrat Congressman Elijah Cummings, who apparently actually colluded directly with the IRS to ensure it targeted conservative groups. In congressional hearings, Catherine Engelbrecht, a conservative activist, Tea Party member, and founder of "True the Vote" testified under oath how Congressman Cummings and multiple government agencies came after her. Cummings sent Mrs.

---

37 Alana Goodman, "Schumer Calls for using IRS to Curtail Tea Party Activities," *Washington Free Beacon*, January 23, 2014, http://freebeacon.com/issues/schumer-calls-for-using-irs-to-curtail-tea-party-activities/.

Engelbrecht four threatening letters and subpoenaed her three times for documents. The threats and intimidation by Congressman Cummings's office reached such a disturbing level that Engelbrecht filed a formal complaint against him with the Office of Congressional Ethics. While that was going on, the power ministries, including the FBI, IRS, ATF, and OSHA, along with the Texas State EPA (more about the EPA office below), descended upon Mrs. Engelbrecht. The IRS opened up *fourteen* separate audits of her personal and business finances, the FBI repeatedly visited her because she was apparently suspected of being a "domestic risk." Also multiple visits from the Bureau of Alcohol Tobacco and Firearms agents, and two audits by the Occupational Safety and Health Administration. Prior to her political advocacy, she had never been on federal radar. However, as soon as she became an activist for her beliefs she found a big target painted on her back.[38]

Cummings's denials that he or his staff had any discussions with the IRS about True the Vote were refuted by numerous e-mails released by the House Oversight Committee, which showed that House Democratic staff requested information from the IRS's tax-exempt division on True The Vote. Cummings officially sought information from True the Vote in October 2012, concurrent with an IRS letter requesting the group provide the agency with copies of its volunteer registration forms and additional information on its volunteer activities. Cummings's staff then requested more information

---

38 Sundance, "The Weaponization of Government – Unbelievable Congressional Testimony on IRS Targeting," *The Conservative Treehouse*, February 6, 2014, http://theconservativetreehouse.com/2014/02/06/the-weaponization-of-government-unbelievable-congressional-testimony-on-irs-targeting/.

from the IRS about True the Vote in January 2013.[39] The request was channeled from the IRS's Legislative Affairs office to several other IRS officials, including Lois Lerner. Three days later, Lerner wrote to her deputy, Holly Paz: "Did we find anything?" Paz wrote that she hadn't heard back, to which Lerner replied: "thanks—check tomorrow please."[40]

True the Vote was just one of hundreds of conservative organizations targeted by the IRS, multiple members of Congress (Cummings, Schumer, and also Senator Sheldon Whitehouse) as well as the Department of Justice. According to the IRS's own internal numbers, they targeted 104 conservative organizations, ultimately approving 46 percent of them. By contrast, only seven liberal groups were questioned, and the IRS approved all of them.[41]

Here is the IRS's mission statement, taken directly from the IRS.gov: "Provide America's taxpayers top quality service by helping them understand and meet their tax responsibilities and enforce the law with integrity and fairness to all." The Internal *Revenue* Service, the agency responsible for making sure that the taxpayer cash keeps rolling in to Washington was not going after these organizations to

---

39 Sundance, "Democrat Congressman Elijah Cummings Caught in "On Record" Committee Lies and Lies to Public through Media – Cummings Colluded with IRS Lois Lerner on Texas Conservative Group," *The Conservative Treehouse*, April 10, 2014, http://theconservativetreehouse.com/2014/04/10/democrat-congressman-elijah-cummings-caught-in-on-record-committee-lies-and-lies-to-public-through-media-cummings-colluded-with-irs-lois-lerner-on-texas-conservative-group/.

40 Susan Ferrechio, "GOP: Justice Department pushed Lois Lerner to help build criminal case against nonprofits," *Washington Examiner*, May 22, 2014, http://washingtonexaminer.com/gop-justice-department-pushed-lerner-to-help-build-criminal-case-against-non-profits/article/2548787.

41 David French, "No, the IRS Did Not Target Conservatives Like it Targeted Conservatives, *National Review*, July 31, 2013, http://www.nationalreview.com/corner/354850/no-irs-did-not-target-progressives-it-targeted-conservatives-david-french.

collect revenue, and they sure as hell weren't operating with "integrity and fairness to all." What they were doing was implementing a carefully planned and coordinated plan to harass, intimidate, and shut down organizations and individuals that were political opponents of the administration in power.

**The EPA: Channeling Attila the Hun**

America is becoming a nanny state. The problem is that the face of our nanny isn't Mary Poppins; it's Attila the Hun, and he isn't taking prisoners. Here's Mr. Al Armendariz, then-chief of the federal government's EPA regional office in Dallas, Texas. Here is how in 2012 he described the EPA's business model:

> It was kind of like how the Romans used to, you know, conquer little villages in the Mediterranean. They'd go into a little Turkish town somewhere, they'd find the first five guys they saw and they would crucify them. And then you know that town was really easy to manage for the next few years.
>
> And so you make examples out of people who are in this case not compliant with the law. Find people who are not compliant with the law, and you hit them as hard as you can and you make examples out of them, and there is a deterrent effect there. And, companies that are smart see that, they don't want to play that game, and they decide at that point that it's time to clean up.
>
> And, that won't happen unless you have somebody out there making examples of people. So you go out, you look at an industry, you find people violating the law, you go aggressively after them. And we do have some pretty effective

> enforcement tools. Compliance can get very high, very, very quickly.
>
> That's what these companies respond to is both their public image but also financial pressure. So you put some financial pressure on a company, you get other people in that industry to clean up very quickly.[42]

No harm, no foul, many will say—just another overzealous bureaucrat trying to make a point. Not so fast. The EPA, along with many other government agencies, has some pretty sharp teeth. According to a 2012 Department of Justice report,[43] some forty federal government agencies, including nearly a dozen not associated with law enforcement such as the EPA, the Bureau of Land Management (BLM), the Fish and Wildlife Service and the Park Service retain over 120,000 paramilitary troops authorized to carry weapons and to make arrests.[44] And they aren't sitting around eating donuts. Examples abound, such as the 2013 EPA armed raid of a tiny mining village of Chicken, Alaska, ostensibly looking for violations of the Clean Water Act; the 2014 standoff between BLM SWAT teams and Nevada cattle rancher Cliven Bundy, because he refused to pay federal cattle "grazing fees"; or the multiple Fish and Wildlife raids on Nashville, Tennessee-based Gibson guitar factories over a three-year period for allegedly using illegally imported wood;

---

42 "EPA Official: EPA's 'philosophy' is to 'crucify' and 'make examples' of US energy producers," *Youtube,* April 25, 2012, https://www.youtube.com/watch?v=ze3GB_b7Nuo

43 Brian Reaves, "Federal Law Enforcement Officers, 2008," U.S. Department of Justice, June 2012, http://www.bjs.gov/content/pub/pdf/fleo08.pdf.

44 "GOP rep wants to cut funding for federal 'paramilitary units' after BLM dispute," *Fox News*, May 1, 2014, http://www.foxnews.com/politics/2014/05/01/gop-rep-wants-to-cut-funding-for-federal-paramilitary-units-after-blm-dispute/.

or federal agents raiding Amish farms at oh-dark-thirty because they were selling "unauthorized" milk.[45]

There's a quote attributed to George Orwell: "People sleep peacefully in their beds at night because rough men stand ready to do violence on their behalf." Those "rough men" to whom he referred were members of our armed forces, an accurate and befitting description. One wonders what Orwell would say about those "rough men" in the Environmental Protection Agency, the Bureau of Land Management, and other regulatory agencies that operate within our borders. On whose behalf, and against whom, are they prepared to do violence?

**Inconvenient Facts**

Where capability and intent converge, action is sure to follow. American politicians and government may not now have the same aggressive intent against its citizens when compared with the Soviet Union, but there is no question that the capability exists here like never before. That's one hell of a lot of trust we are now required to have in our government. Moreover, there is no question that United States is far removed from the nation of constitutionally

**Federal Government Land Ownership**

As of 2008, the federal government had claimed approximately 30 percent of the country for its own. Why does the government own so much land? The top ten list of states with the highest percentage of federally owned land: http://bigthink.com/strange-maps/291-federal-lands-in-the-us

- Nevada 84.5%
- Alaska 69.1%
- Utah 57.4%
- Oregon 53.1%
- Idaho 50.2%
- Arizona 48.1%
- California 45.3%
- Wyoming 42.3%
- New Mexico 41.8%
- Colorado 36.6%

45 Snyder, "12 Ridiculous Government Regulations," #6, *Business Insider* http://www.businessinsider.com/ridiculous-regulations-big-government-2010-11?slop=1#6-raw-milk-license-6.

limited government and individual liberty that we were designed to be. So in which direction is America headed? At the end of the previous chapter there was a section called "Government-Sponsored Civil Unrest" that foresees what is in store for Americans when the government, upon which its citizens have become so reliant, can no longer meet its commitments and promises to the tune of about $100 trillion. While you are thinking about that, ask yourself if you are comfortable with the federal government funding, arming, and training an army of over 120,000 troops, assigning them to domestic regulatory agencies, and giving them the authority to raid homes and businesses of American citizens. Are you comfortable watching the IRS operate in conjunction with the FBI, OSHA, the Department of Justice, and members of Congress in order to openly target individuals and groups, US citizens all, who are perceived to be a political threat to the current administration? Are you comfortable that your entire life is a few gigabytes of memory permanently stored and forever accessible in some government database? Does it bother you when your elected representatives openly ignore, even violate, their oath to support and defend the Constitution? Are you comfortable with the fact that the federal government has quietly seized more than one-third of America's land?

These are all "inconvenient facts" that should be of concern to all Americans, regardless of political stripe, because it's going to get worse before it gets better. Future administrations and members of Congress, regardless of party, will pocket all of the power grabs of previous administrations and expand upon them. That is the inevitable component of human nature the Founders sought to mitigate by designing a limited government. But limited government, separation of powers, individual liberty, and free markets only work when political leaders play by the rules. So as we move closer to a potential clash of civil unrest against a weaponized government, where is America headed: individual liberty or government tyranny?

# CHAPTER 4

# Rebooting Government with an Article V Convention of States

What should be manifestly clear by now is that our government and the career politicians in Congress who benefit from it *are* the problem. Our government is a weaponized parasite that is feeding upon the wealth, productivity, and liberty of its host—us. It didn't happen overnight; it took some time to get here, but it is the inevitable consequence of turning away from limited government and individual liberty as provided for in the Constitution.Instead, the politics of progressivism have put America on the cusp of becoming a cradle-to-grave social welfare state. Government-driven social justice and forced income redistribution might sound good to some, but it is taking America to a very dark place with $17-plus trillion of debt, $100 trillion in unfunded mandates, a perpetually stagnant economy with little or no GDP growth, mountains of regulations, and a dearth of individual liberty. Riding high on the coattails of America's government-gone-wild are the career politicians of both political parties, who, as we've seen, benefit from and facilitate the expansion of government power and authority, and they are harder to get rid of than cockroaches. Democrats openly seek a nanny state, and establishment Republicans, despite their rhetoric, also support and gain from big government. We are being overrun, and there's nowhere to turn—no dramatic election cycle, no party takeover of Congress or the White house; no new politician is going to fix Washington and begin the work of restoring America's core principles of limited government, individual liberty, and free markets. The only way to accomplish that is to reboot Washington from the outside. That means changing the conditions on the political battlefield. This chapter explains how we can accomplish that through enacting two key constitutional amendments through an Article V Convention of States.

**Article V of the US Constitution**

> The Congress, whenever two thirds of both Houses shall deem it necessary, shall propose Amendments to this Constitution, or, on the Application of the Legislatures of two thirds of the several States, shall call a Convention for proposing Amendments, which, in either Case, shall be valid to all Intents and Purposes, as Part of this Constitution, when ratified by the Legislatures of three fourths of the several States, or by Conventions in three fourths thereof, as the one or the other Mode of Ratification may be proposed by the Congress; Provided that no Amendment which may be made prior to the Year One thousand eight hundred and eight shall in any Manner affect the first and fourth Clauses in the Ninth Section of the first Article; and that no State, without its Consent, shall be deprived of its equal Suffrage in the Senate.

**Breaking Down Article V**

Article V of the Constitution provides two avenues to propose amendments to the Constitution. The first, most direct, and what has always been used, is for two-thirds of both houses of Congress to propose amendments: *The Congress, whenever two thirds of both*

*Houses shall deem it necessary, shall propose Amendments to this Constitution ...*

The second method, never used, is nonetheless equally valid. It calls for the legislatures of two-thirds of the states (that's thirty-four today) to submit applications calling for a convention for proposing amendments: ... *or, on the Application of the Legislatures of two thirds of the several States, shall call a Convention for proposing Amendments ...*

Both options then require ratification by three-fourths (that's thirty-eight today) of state legislatures or state ratifying conventions: *which, in either Case, shall be valid to all Intents and Purposes, as Part of this Constitution, when ratified by the Legislatures of three fourths of the several States, or by Conventions in three fourths thereof ...*

## Why There Are Two Methods to Propose Constitutional Amendments

Why did the founders include two methods to amend the Constitution? Why not just let the US Congress propose amendments? That is certainly easier and more direct than the "herding cats" option of getting two-thirds of the state legislatures to act in concert. The answer to this is as telling as it is timely. As discussed throughout this book, the founders did not trust government and those in charge to forever remain benign. They deliberately installed numerous horizontal and vertical constraints by way of the separation of powers and empowering states. Allowing for a Convention of States in Article V is a key component of that. In fact we have Colonel George Mason of Virginia to thank for the convention clause. During the Constitutional Convention of 1787, Mason voiced his concerns about what could happen if the federal government and Congress became oppressive and too powerful. Mason argued that it "would be improper to require the consent of the Natl. Legislature, because they may abuse their power, and refuse their consent on that very account." Mason then added that, "no amendments of the proper kind would ever be obtained by the people, if the Government should become oppressive."[46] He therefore insisted upon a workaround, a trapdoor of sorts, that America could fall back on if and when the federal government became oppressive. In response to Mason's concerns, the convention concurred and unanimously voted to add the language allowing states to apply to Congress for a convention to propose amendments to the Constitution. The power behind Mason's clause is that it takes the amendment process out of the hands of Congress and the federal government and puts it in the hands of "We, the people." It changes the conditions on the political battlefield. Washington is the source of the problems facing us today, and it will never self-limit. That was Mason's fear in 1787; today it has become our reality.

## The Process of Convening an Article V Convention of States

Calling a convention would be a challenging process even under the best of circumstances. The 1787 version was a tall order to organize, and given the tawdry state of affairs inside our current political process, it will be every bit as challenging as the original. Per the Article V process, state legislatures must submit applications to Congress, whereupon critical mass of thirty-four states is reached, a convention may go forward. In fact hundreds of applications have dribbled in to Congress from the states at one time or another dating all the way back to 1788. They address an array of potential amendments on relevant issues of their period such as slavery, antipolygamy, repeal of the Sixteenth and Eighteenth Amendments, right to life, a balanced budget, and congressional term limits. The issue surrounding a recent movement that has seen significant momentum

---

46 Russell Caplan, *Constitutional Brinksmanship, Amending the Constitution by National Convention*, (New York: Oxford, 1988), 29.

was on holding a convention explicitly to enact a balanced budget amendment. Arguably thirty-four states submitted applications, but a few of those states subsequently rescinded their applications, leaving the actual total of thirty-four in doubt. Moreover, the wording of the applications varied, which further detracted from the process.

This underlines a critical challenge in bringing a convention to fruition. While the Congress has no say in the drafting and ratifying of amendments once the convention is convened, it is Congress that "shall call a Convention" in order for it to begin. Since it is quite clear that Congress has no intention to self-limit its ability to spend money *vis a vis* a balanced budget amendment or to curtail Members' own longevity through term limits, it follows that any and all discrepancies in states' applications will enable Congress to avoid calling a convention. Additionally, getting thirty-four individual states on the same sheet of music will be a monumental exercise of herding cats. A successful effort will take some central organization and oversight, combined with sustained grassroots efforts in each state. My recommendations for that are found below in the section "Two Key Principles of War: Objective and Unity of Command."

Once at least thirty-four states have submitted applications to Congress, the Constitution says that Congress *shall* call a convention. Each state would then choose its delegates to represent that state at the convention. Amendments would be proposed, debated, and voted upon at the convention. It has been noted that each state can send as many delegates as it wishes, but each state will get one overall vote in the convention. This book, for example, calls for two critical amendments: congressional term limits and a balanced budget amendment. However, a convention likely would be more expansive. In his book *The Liberty Amendments,* Mark Levin, an unapologetic conservative well known across radio air waves, proposes eleven amendments designed to "Restore the American Republic," which also happens to be the book's subtitle. Once each amendment passes in the convention, three-fourths of the states (thirty-eight) would then be needed for the amendment to be ratified and become law.

**Conflicting Viewpoints—Arguments Against a Convention of States**

There are a number of concerns from across the political spectrum about a convention. Clearly, progressives would fight tooth and nail against efforts to limit government according to what is proposed herein, so pushback from the Left is largely predictable and expected (there is, however, some desire from the tinfoil wing of the Democrat Party to convene a convention of states, more on this below). There is also pushback from some conservative individuals and groups. These include a number of sitting Republican politicians (I rest my case), academicians, judges, and organizations such as the John Birch Society and the Eagle Forum. Their arguments against calling a convention vary according to their own interests and focus.

One major concern from the Right is the potential of a "runaway" convention, whereby bad actors, be it the likes of George Soros, the ACLU, or the Service Employee International Union (SEIU), would somehow fund and facilitate a convention takeover and push through major rewrites of the Constitution that would take away freedoms and compromise US sovereignty. What if, some worry, states decided to choose as their delegate Nancy Pelosi or Harry Reid or Elizabeth Warren? As mentioned above, indeed there have been proposals from Leftist groups for a convention that entertains notions along the lines of "internationalizing" the Constitution, repealing the Second Amendment, "downgrading" freedom of religion from a right to a privilege, eliminating free markets and transforming the nation into a *de jure* social welfare state. Recently an Occupy Wall Street spinoff political action committee called Wolf PAC has called for an amendment to prohibit corporations and unions from making campaign contributions. However, it is important to remember that delegates are chosen by, and tethered to, their respective states. Each state has the ability to select its own delegates to the convention, and may also recall them if they do not adhere to their instructions. My initial gut reaction to this concern was that if representatives from thirty-four states would deliberately propose destructive, anti-American amendments along the lines of these, not to mention finding thirty-eight states to ratify them, then we are already too far gone as a nation to salvage the Constitution. I simply refuse to believe this could be the case. Will bad actors attempt to push for whacky amendments in the event that there is a convention of states? Without a doubt. But the day we start cutting and running from the likes of Soros, Pelosi, or the SEIU is the day we no longer deserve to call ourselves Americans.

Another argument from conservatives is that a convention, even if held and good amendments proposed and ratified, won't matter, because if Congress and the government refuse to adhere to the Constitution now, why would they do so after a convention? The best response to this comes from the organization "Convention of States:"

> When the founders wrote the Constitution, they did not anticipate modern-day politicians who take advantage of loopholes and vague phraseology. Even though it is obvious to all reasonable Americans that the federal government is violating the original meaning of the Constitution, Washington pretends otherwise, claiming the Constitution contains broad and flexible language. Amendments at a Convention of States today will be written with the current state of the federal government in mind. The language they use for these amendments will be unequivocal. There will be no doubt as to their meaning, no possibility of alternate interpretations,

> and no way for them to be legitimately broken. In addition to this, it should be noted that the federal government has not violated the amendments passed in recent years. Women's suffrage, for example, has been 100% upheld."[47]

It is also worth noting that implementing congressional term limits will do away with career politicians who, term after term, are able to build their own empires, amass millions of dollars in campaign funds, and insulate themselves from any accountability. This does not mean that a term-limited member of Congress, particularly one of the progressive flavor, might still attempt to ignore the Constitution, but the dynamic will have been changed. Moreover, with term limits, he or she would soon be gone.

One commonality shared by all of the conservative opponents to a Convention of States is that they have no viable alternatives to offer other than to maintain the status quo. Opponents tend to agree with the core principles of limited government and individual liberty, but the only arrow in their quiver is to "stay the course," continue to operate within the current political paradigm and hope that things will somehow eventually get better. How's that working for us now? As I pointed out in the introduction of this book, "hope" isn't a strategy.

## Two Key Principles of War: Objective and Unity of Command

This section amounts to a little inside baseball for getting to an Article V Convention of States. There are a number of Article V movements at present, which underscores the widespread discomfort coursing throughout the nation and the accompanying realization that government is the principal source of our problems. Some organizations, such as

---

47 *Convention of States*, https://d3n8a8pro7vhmx.cloudfront.net/conventionofstates/pages/145/attachments/original/1410015573/Frequently-Asked-Questions_01.pdf?1410015573.

the Balanced Budget Amendment Task Force, are amendment-specific Article V movements. Other groups, such as the Convention of States, seek a convention without advocating for or against any specific amendment. Appendix 1 provides an extensive list of active movements; if I missed any (and I'm sure I have; they are legion), it probably wasn't intentional. However, the plethora of movements seeking to have states submit their applications to Congress is also a potential detriment. I'll explain why by returning to my professional military roots. The US Army's Field Manual 3-0, entitled "Operations" details nine separate and distinct principles of war. These are the army's rendition of timeless characteristics that are common to successful military operations. Two of them are particularly relevant for our purposes here.

> **Objective**: Direct every military operation toward a clearly defined, decisive and attainable objective.

Too many separate organizations lobbying state legislators across the country to adopt assorted and disparate applications is detrimental. It dilutes the overall effort and will only confuse and divide the state legislators, who must support one or another version of the applications that are being put in front of them. It could even divide legislators who might otherwise be united in the concept of convening a convention of states. Therefore the process should be streamlined to make it as transparent and simple as possible for the legislators to vote to submit an application to Congress. Moreover, as I pointed out above, Congress, which must call a convention once thirty-four applications are received, will take any opportunity and use any excuse to avoid having to call a convention. That includes getting applications that call for one amendment or another (remember, states have submitted applications for conventions on a plethora of different amendments). When a critical mass of thirty-four applications is achieved, those applications should be uniform and speak with one voice. Thus the separate and distinct movements, most of which are laudable in their desire to restore the Constitution, actually detract from convening a convention of states. It is a tactical issue. Obtaining thirty-four viable applications is, to paraphrase our principle of war above, a "*clearly defined, decisive and obtainable objective*." This brings us to our second principle of war, unity of command.

> **Unity of Command**: For every objective, ensure unity of effort under one responsible commander. Applying a force's full combat power requires unity of command. Unity of command means that a single commander directs and coordinates the actions of all forces toward a common objective. Cooperation may produce coordination, but giving a single commander the required authority is the most effective way to achieve unity of effort.

I believe it is essential that there be some central leadership and organization coordinating efforts at the grassroots level in each state and the lobbying efforts within respective state legislatures. One organization that has the capacity to accomplish this is the Convention of States. This is a project that was started by the Citizens for Self Government, one of the prime movers behind and founders of the Tea Party Patriots. I believe this organization has two critical advantages that best position it to accomplish the objective. First, the group comes prepackaged with a massive, broad-based grassroots organization at hand stemming from its Tea Party efforts. Having an existing army of boots on the ground in virtually every state is a huge advantage. Second, the Convention of States offers a single application that calls for a convention for the purpose of limiting the power and jurisdiction of the federal government. It does not advocate for or against any specific constitutional amendment. This approach takes away any ambiguity and deprives the US Congress of any wiggle room to avoid calling a convention once thirty-four applications are submitted. This does not in any way render other organizations redundant. On the contrary, unification of effort under a central command would be a force multiplier: "Cooperation may produce coordination, but giving a single commander the required authority is the most effective way to achieve unity of effort."

We could also file this under another, unofficial principle often cited in the military; the KISS method, which stands for Keep It Simple, Stupid. Orchestrating a Convention of States is going to be hard enough; a clearly identified objective combined with a well-coordinated effort up front will result in a smoother Convention.

## Restoring America, Part One: Eliminating Career Politicians with Congressional Term Limits

Chapter 2 explained how career politicians of both parties perpetuate and expand government in order to protect their incumbencies, which is clearly their overriding priority. As recently as 2012, then Senator Jim DeMint (R, SC) put forward a nonbinding "sense of the Senate" proposal that the Constitution "ought" to be amended to place limits on how long members of Congress could serve. It was defeated 75–24.[48] Members of Congress will never voluntarily pass anything that will limit their tenure. Therefore it is up to us to put limits on them by limiting the number of terms they can serve. This has

**States with Strict Term Limits Are Also the Most Cash Solvent**

We can look to the states for examples of what happens with term limits. TermLimits.org cites a 2014 Mercatus Center at George Mason University study, "State Fiscal Condition: Ranking the 50 States," which reveals that four of the top five most cash-solvent states — Ohio, South Dakota, Florida, and Montana — have strict, eight-year term limits. By contrast, the state that finished dead last in cash solvency was Illinois, the one state without term limits.[49]

[48] Josiah Ryan, "Senate rejects term limits in 24-75 vote," *The Hill*, February 2, 2012, http://thehill.com/blogs/floor-action/senate/208395-senate-rejects-amendment-recommending-congressional-term-limit-.

been proven to work at the state level, particularly with regard to fiscal responsibility.

My proposal:

Senate: a maximum of two six-year terms
House: a maximum of five two-year terms

A maximum of twelve years in the Senate and ten years in the House is sufficient to make an impact and fulfill campaign promises. There is something to be said for "learning the ropes," but if it takes more than a couple of months to catch on, then you probably don't have any business being in Congress in the first place. That is certainly the case with many politicians who never seem to get it but who just won't go away. Congresswoman Sheila Jackson-Lee from Texas has been in Congress for twenty years, ostensibly upholding the Constitution, a document that she seems to know very little about. In March 2014 she said the following:

> Maybe I should offer a good thanks to the distinguished members of the majority, the Republicans, my chairman and others, for giving us an opportunity to have a deliberative constitutional discussion that reinforces the sanctity of this nation and how well it is that we have lasted some 400 years, operating under a Constitution that clearly defines what is constitutional and what is not."[50]

So according to Congresswoman Jackson-Lee, the United States and our Constitution came into being somewhere around 1614. Apparently that

---

49 Nick Tomboulides, "States with Eight-Year Term Limits are the Most Cash Solvent," *U.S. Term Limits*, March 12, 2014, https://termlimits.org/states-eight-year-term-limits-cash-solvent/

50 Cheryl Chumley, "Rep. Sheila Jackson Lee claims Constitution is 400 years old," *Washington Times*, March 13, 2014, http://www.washingtontimes.com/news/2014/mar/13/sheila-jackson-lee-claims-constitution-400-years-o/.

Constitutional Convention of 1787 in Philadelphia was just for show. Or something. I don't know about you, but I'd like for my representative in Congress to at least get the century right. Ms. Jackson-Lee, along with many others in Congress, is a walking, talking advertisement for term limits.

There should also be some additional limits on members of Congress in order to ensure that they legislate on behalf of their constituents and not themselves. Serving in Congress should be treated as a duty and an honor, not a boondoggle. For example:

- Congressional salaries and benefits are capped and all pay raises (including COLA) require a three-fourths majority and must be publicly announced and justified by leaders of both parties.
- All personal investments must be placed in a blind trust and cannot be viewed or accessed from swearing in until leaving office.

**Restoring America, Part Two: Reining in Big Government with a Balanced Budget Amendment**

Chapter 3 detailed how the US government is now a zero-sum threat to the liberty and productivity of its own citizenry and is destroying the American dream for our children and future generations. The federal government, designed to be extremely limited in nature, has become a greedy parasite that can only sustain and expand by consuming its host—the wealth, productivity, and liberty of the citizens it was created to serve. Moreover, the government has weaponized itself to control the population, to ensure that the revenue continues to flow in, that endless regulations are obeyed, and that political opposition is intimidated. This is in direct contravention of the Constitution and of the principles of limited government, individual liberty, and free markets that are the bedrock of American exceptionalism. This massive, unconstitutional expansion of government was only possible with the funding that came from the Sixteenth Amendment in 1913, which legalized the federal income tax. Taxpayer dollars, combined with government-friendly progressive politics, have been the catalyst for the growth of the federal government. It has also opened the door for career politicians of both parties to spend trillions of tax dollars expanding government and to keep themselves in power. Congress and the government have already overspent by over $17 trillion, and they have overpromised (i.e., unfunded mandates) to the tune of almost $100 trillion. There isn't enough money in the world to pay for that, yet that is what our government is going to owe in the coming years. Easy money and zero accountability have been the formula, so it follows that by capping their ability to spend our money, it becomes possible to gradually wrestle big government to the mat. That is why a balanced budget amendment to the Constitution is essential if America is to return to its core principles.

**Jefferson Quote**

To preserve our independence, we must not let our rulers load us with perpetual debt. I wish it were possible to obtain a single amendment to our Constitution ... an additional article, taking from the federal government the power of borrowing,

—Thomas Jefferson

A balanced budget amendment must be very specific so that Congress cannot evade it. A balanced budget amendment should include the following:

- Total government outlays cannot exceed tax receipts for a given fiscal year.
- Any budget surplus must go toward debt reduction.
- Total government outlays cannot exceed 18 percent of the national GDP.

- Individual tax rates should not exceed 15 percent of income.
- The president must submit a balanced budget to Congress, and Congress must pass a balanced budget prior to the beginning of the fiscal year. If this does not happen, it should trigger automatic budget reductions from the previous year's budget.
- The entire federal budget should be discretionary. Entitlement programs should be taken off of autopilot and pooled with all other spending (this will force Congress to pursue entitlement reform).
- Emergency clause to violate any components of this amendment must be done on an annual basis and be approved by a two-thirds roll call vote of both chambers.

**Admiral Mullen Quote**

I've said many times that I believe the single, biggest threat to our national security is our debt.

—Admiral Mike Mullen, former chairman of the Joint Chiefs of Staff

While there have been recent balanced budget amendment proposals surfacing in Congress, they did not come close to passing, and were likely for show. Here are the CRS summaries of both:

Sponsored by Senator Orrin Hatch (R, UT) in 2011:

Constitutional Amendment—Prohibits outlays for a fiscal year (except those for repayment of debt principal) from exceeding total receipts for that fiscal year (except those derived from borrowing) unless Congress, by a two-thirds roll call vote of each chamber, authorizes a specific excess of outlays over receipts.

Prohibits total outlays for any fiscal year from exceeding 20 % of the gross domestic product for the preceding calendar year unless Congress, by a two-thirds roll call vote of each chamber, authorizes a specific excess over such 20%.

Directs the President to submit a balanced budget to Congress annually.

Prohibits any bill to increase federal taxes from becoming law unless approved by two-thirds of each chamber by roll call vote.

Authorizes waivers of these provisions when a declaration of war is in effect or under other specified circumstances involving military conflict.

Sponsored by Rep. Bob Goodlatte (R, VA) in 2011:

Constitutional Amendment—Prohibits total outlays for a fiscal year (except those for repayment of debt principal) from exceeding total receipts for that fiscal year (except those derived from borrowing) unless Congress, by a three-fifths roll call vote of each chamber, authorizes a specific excess of outlays over receipts.

Requires a three-fifths roll call vote of each chamber to increase the public debt limit.

Directs the President to submit a balanced budget to Congress annually.

Prohibits any bill to increase revenue from becoming law unless approved by a majority of each chamber by roll call vote.

Authorizes waivers of these provisions when a declaration of war is in effect or under other specified circumstances involving military conflict. Requires any such waiver to identify and be limited to the specific excess or increase for that fiscal year made necessary by the identified military conflict.

## Conclusion

Term limits and a balanced budget amendment will begin the work of restoring America by returning our nation to those core principles of limited government and individual liberty. This will ignite an explosion of private sector productivity, job growth, wealth creation, and economic opportunity unlike what any American has experienced since the Reagan years. Tragically, these measures will never come close to the two-thirds vote necessary to pass in Congress; they will never voluntarily give up the immense power they have amassed. It is going to be up to us.

# CHAPTER 5

# The Third American Wave

*Governments are instituted among Men, deriving their just powers from the consent of the governed,—That whenever any Form of Government becomes destructive of these ends, it is the Right of the People to alter or abolish it, and to institute new Government.*
—Excerpt from the Declaration of Independence, July 4, 1776

Earlier I described America's evolution as coming out of two seismic historical waves:

**The First American Wave: The Revolutionary War**

It is truly amazing how history repeats. Take a minute to reread the excerpt from the Declaration of Independence above. Sound familiar? The oppressive government that they faced back in the summer of 1776 is precisely where we find ourselves today, with a government that is "*destructive of these ends*." We know how they reacted in 1776, and we know that it culminated in our Constitution and the founding of what would become the greatest nation in history. It was the First American Wave.

## The Second American Wave: The Civil War

Almost a century later, the Second American Wave came. The Civil War tore America apart, only to ultimately remake it whole again, and better than it was before. Distilled down to its essence, it was about another passage found in the Declaration of Independence: "We hold these truths to be self-evident, *that all men are created equal.*" The Civil War, the Second American Wave, put paid to those six words. It brought about the Thirteenth, Fourteenth, and Fifteenth Amendments to the Constitution. The truth and the beauty of that document and the price paid from 1776 to 1865 is manifested, among other things, in the fact that in 2008 Americans chose a black man as their president.

## The Third American Wave on the Horizon: The Demise of America or a Rebirth?

Looking back on these seismic historical events through the large end of the telescope where we know the outcome, it is easy to gloss over the sacrifices those men and women made, the hardship and the losses they endured in fighting for those causes in which they believed. In the throes of those events they surely did not know what the outcome was going to be, whether those respective wars would be won or lost, and what the ramifications would be. Indeed, success was far from certain; both the Revolutionary War and the Civil War could just have easily been lost. Had one or the other failed, the United States of America would have a very different look and feel today, if it existed at all. In the end, both were successful thanks to those Americans who stood up for what they believed, from leaders such as George Washington and Abraham Lincoln, to the foot soldiers in the mud who had the will and the courage to see it through.

Now in the twenty-first century a Third American Wave is on the horizon. This wave has the potential to crush the American dream under the weight of unresolvable debt, and regulations that strangle the free market and constrict our individual liberty. It is a wave created by an oppressive, parasitic government that is consuming its host; you and I. Therefore it follows that it is the right—the duty—of We, the People, to alter that government that has once again become so "*destructive of these ends*." That means changing the conditions on the political battlefield. It means a nationwide grassroots movement, state by state, culminating in an Article V, George Mason-inspired convention of states. It means not stopping until amendments for a balanced budget and for congressional term limits are adopted in the Constitution. And it needs to happen very soon, before America is overrun.

**Powerful Adversaries**

Be warned, this is going to take a fight. This is not a prediction or an advocacy an armed conflict, but make no mistake, there will be massive opposition to any viable movement to change the big government status quo. It means that those inside the Beltway who have amassed a great deal of power, wealth, and authority, will not willingly give this up, and they are either blind or indifferent to the damage it is doing across the country. The vast majority of the professional political class in Washington, as well as the legions of government bureaucrats, consultants, lobbyists, and political party operatives will not go gently into that good night. The Democrat Party will fight this tooth and nail; they're on the cusp of completing the exacta of a government-led social welfare state combined with a command administrative economy. The establishment wing of the Republican Party will also resist; they're not so worried about big government as long as they are in charge of it. The fear mongering about a "runaway convention" as described in chapter 4 of this book is largely promulgated by establishment Republicans. I am infinitely more concerned about the runaway Congress that is here now.

Nothing worthwhile comes easy. Where would we be if George Washington had looked at regiment after regiment of heavily armed Redcoats, backed up by the powerful Royal Navy, and decided that resistance was just going to be too hard, that a war was unwinnable, and instead the Colonists should just reason with King George III and hope that everything would work out for the best? Or if Abraham Lincoln had caved to his critics, including many in his own party, who said that a war against the Confederacy should not be fought and/or couldn't be won, and that perhaps he should just let the southern states go their own way? Or if America's Greatest Generation had witnessed the Nazi *Blitzkrieg* at work and decided that any war against them was unwinnable, and that it was really a European problem anyway? If we delay because this mission of convening a convention of states seems too difficult, if we listen to the naysayers or those who would keep things the way they are, or we just sit back and "hope" (that word again) that the government and career politicians will at some point voluntarily self-limit, we and future generations will be overrun.

## Powerful Allies

Now it is our turn. Despite the obstacles, a convention of states is the right thing to do if we are to save our nation and restore the American dream. And while we have powerful opposition, we also have even more powerful allies. Who are they? America's founding documents, the Constitution and the Declaration of Independence, are on our side. The Founding Fathers, who believed in limited government and individual liberty, are on our side. Those who acknowledge the uniqueness, the exceptionalism of America and the American Dream are on our side. Those willing to confront tyranny and oppression at home and abroad are on our side. Those who support the need to maintain a powerful military, those who understand the nature of "Peace through Strength," are on our side. Veterans, those men and women who have served this nation, who put their lives on the line, and who swore an oath to "support and defend the Constitution against all enemies, foreign and domestic," are on our side. Future generations of Americans, born and unborn, who would pursue the American dream are very much on our side. And finally, if you believe, like our founders did, that the unalienable rights of life, liberty, and the pursuit of happiness are endowed, not by governments, but by our Creator, then it follows that in this endeavor *we* are on the side of the Creator.

**Your Country Needs You**

Our country does not run on autopilot. Just like a marriage, a garden, a home, or an automobile, everything in life worth having requires careful attention, nurturing, and protection and support. The United States of America is no different, and if we take our blessings of liberty for granted, we *will* lose them. Ronald Reagan put it best:

> Freedom is never more than one generation away from extinction. We didn't pass it to our children in the bloodstream. It must be fought for, protected, and handed on for them to do the same, or one day we will spend our sunset years telling our children and our children's children what it was once like in the United States where men were free.

And that is where we find ourselves today, living in a nation that is being overrun by an out of control government. If there is going to be an America left to hand down to our children, it is up to us to fight for and protect this country, to support and defend the Constitution. An

Article V Convention of States is an instrument specifically designed for the situation in which we now find ourselves.

So sign up and volunteer with one or more of these organizations; there are never enough boots on the ground. If you can, donate a little money; every little bit helps. Think of it as an investment in your country and your future. It might turn into the best investment you'll ever make. Besides, most of those organizations are 501(C)(3) non-profits, so any contribution is tax deductible, which beats sending your hard-earned money to Washington. Veterans, this cause is right in your wheelhouse; you've taken the oath to support and defend the Constitution against all enemies, foreign and domestic, and that's what this is about. Citizens, if you love this country, value your liberty, your possessions, and your kids, this is your fight too.

The contact info you need to enlist is included in the appendix. Also, please contact your state representative directly. Ask that person what their position is regarding a convention of states as allowed by Article V of the Constitution. Tell that representative if he or she wants your support, you expect him or her to support a convention of states. Remember, your representative works for you. We've got this.

# ABOUT THE AUTHOR

Patrick Murray is a retired US Army colonel. His military career took him out of his native Oklahoma to exotic destinations throughout the world, operating in diverse cultures and missions. He commanded tank units astride the Fulda Gap, staring down Soviet forces just across the border. Soon after, he found himself on the other side of that border, living and working in Moscow for the Defense Intelligence Agency. Patrick worked in numerous US embassies, including as a military attaché in Belgrade, Yugoslavia, during the Balkans conflict. He was part of a military-political exchange program, assigned alongside American diplomats at the State Department in Washington, DC. Later he became the US representative to the Military Staff Committee at the United Nations in New York. During the Iraq War "surge" of 2007, he deployed to Baghdad. Patrick holds degrees from Oklahoma State University and The Ohio State University, is a graduate of the Command and General Staff College and the Defense Language Institute, where he studied Russian. He has also been a guest lecturer at the Army War College. Patrick often says that there is no statute of limitations on the oath he took to "support and defend the Constitution," so after the army, he sought to continue serving the nation in a different venue. He ran for US Congress in Virginia, where he was twice the Republican nominee. Patrick lives and works in Old Town Alexandria, where he enjoys jogging and biking along the Potomac River and volunteers for his pet causes, including the Board of Directors for Virginia Veterans' Affairs and the local Animal Welfare League. He is a writer and political and foreign policy commentator, and is president and CEO of Third Wave Communications. You can follow his musings on ExceptionalAmerica.net.

# APPENDIX: SOURCE FILE OF LINKS

A listing of selected organizations calling for a Convention of States.

https://conventionofstates.com

http://www.callaconvention.org

http://www.foavc.org

http://www.termlimitsforuscongress.com

https://termlimits.org

http://www.bba4usa.org

http://balancedbudgetamendmentnow.com

http://www.article5.org

http://www.article-v-convention.com

# SELECTED BIBLIOGRAPHY

Alinsky, Saul. *Rules for Radicals*. New York: Random House, 1971.

Bowen, Catherine Drinker. *Miracle at Philadelphia: The Story of the Constitutional Convention*. Boston: Little, Brown, 1966.

Brookhiser, Richard. *Founding Father: Rediscovering George Washington*. New York: Free Press, 1996.

Carleson, Robert. *Government Is the Problem: Memoirs of Ronald Reagan's Welfare Reformer*. Alexandria: American Civil Rights Union, 2009.

D'Souza, Dinesh. *America: Imagine a World Without Her*. Washington, DC: Regnery, 2014.

De Tocqueville, Alexis. *Democracy in America*. New York: Alfred A. Knopf, 1972.

Ellis, Joseph. *American Creation: Triumphs and Tragedies at the Founding of the Republic*. New York: Alfred A. Knopf, 2007.

Folsom, Burton. *New Deal or Raw Deal? How FDR's Economic Legacy Has Damaged America*. New York: Threshold Editions, 2008.

Friedman, Milton. *Capitalism and Freedom*. Chicago: University of Chicago Press, 2002.

———. *Why Government Is the Problem*. Stanford: Hoover Institution Press, 1993.

Hayek, Friedrich. *The Road to Serfdom*. London: University of Chicago Press, 2007.

Levin, Mark. *The Liberty Amendments*. New York: Threshold Editions, 2013.

Mamet, David. *The Secret Knowledge: On the Dismantling of American Culture*._New York: Penguin, 201.

Pestritto, Ronald. *Woodrow Wilson and the Roots of Modern Liberalism*. New York: Rowman & Littlefield, 2005.

Reagan, Ronald. *An American Life*. New York: Threshold Editions, 1990.

Schweizer, Peter. *Extortion: How Politicians Extract Your Money, Buy Votes and Line Their Own Pockets*. New York: Houghton Mifflin, 2013.

———. *Throw Them All Out: How Politicians and Their Friends Get Rich off Insider Stock Tips, Land Deals, and Cronyism that Would Send the Rest of Us to Prison*. New York: Houghton Mifflin, 2011.

Skousen, W. Cleon. *The Five Thousand Year Leap: 28 Great Ideas that Changed the World*. Franklin: American Documents Publishing, 2009.

The Federalist Papers

The Constitution of the United States

The Declaration of Independence

Printed in the United States
By Bookmasters